Never Alone—Until Admiral Halsey Left...with Everyone Else

◆

Personal Involvement—with Typhoons,
Filth, Cannibalism, and Body Parts in the

Biggest War of All Times

◆

by

Harrison E. Lemont

DORRANCE PUBLISHING CO., INC.
PITTSBURGH, PENNSYLVANIA 15222

ISBN # 0-8059-6025-2
Printed in the United States of America

First Printing

For information or to order additional books, please write:
Dorrance Publishing Co., Inc.
701 Smithfield Street
Third Floor
Pittsburgh, Pennsylvania 15222
U.S.A.
1-800-788-7654
Or visit our web site and on-line catalog at *www.dorrancepublishing.com*

To my friend, my companion, my buddy, Bernard Gross,
who made those war years tolerable.

◆

Acknowledgments

If it had not been for the encouragement and assistance of many, this book would never have been written.

When I first entered the military service, I had thought I might some day write about the war and my experiences and so, I kept notes in a diary. Unfortunately, it was not kept as a diary per se, with feelings and emotions, but more as a record. But it does help in identifying times and places.

However it was not until I started taking writing courses, seeing and hearing the reaction of fellow students and teachers to accounts of my war experiences, that I felt that maybe a book could be a reality. It was, as many of them said, "something that should be told." They had never heard or even knew about the daily, routine side of war—what the individual soldier endures.

Much thanks goes to Nancy Lamire, my first writing teacher, who was very encouraging, reaffirming that what I had experienced had to be told. To Dawn Haines, who was so helpful in teaching me so much, explaining to me how to show more and tell less, demanding that it was not acceptable to say that a thing was difficult to describe: "You must try! It's your job!" I learned from her how to find the right shape, voice, and tense for each piece of writing. Ron Mills—an editor by occupation—graciously, through editing a couple of chapters, showed me how best to reshape the book. My fellow classmates—Peggy Elliott, Marlane Bottino, Peg Sullivan, Jo Ann Beaudette, Barbara and Gary Boggiano, and Diane Sawyer—through questions and suggestions, were of great assistance.

Thanks also to my family: wife Arline; sons Kenneth and Andrew; daughter-in-law Gail; and grandsons Keith and Eric, who were very supportive, reading much of my work and tolerating my interrogations. And a special acknowledgment to all the members of F Platoon, 727 SAW Company, for being my companions, my comrades, my family during those horrendous years.

Introduction

Under constant threat from a fanatic enemy, with many dead all around; daily challenges; little sleep under difficult conditions; hot, humid days; days of constant rain; periods with little to eat, youthful laughter, games, and sports—these are my scattered pictures of war.

From the ship-crowded beaches on Leyte Gulf to Ormoc's sweltering horror; from flying to fighting-intense Okinawa to being isolated on coral Tori Shima to bombs, torpedoes, filth, insects, tornadoes, rifle fire, rodents—coping with ever-present danger was a daily challenge. Yet in spite of how we had to live, we were of that young, indestructible age, adjusting to each day's new obstacles. Within our group, there never was a fight or even a harsh word.

In a letter home while we were in the Ormoc area, which was a very low point in my life, an excerpt from it stated, "But there's the brighter side, the adventure, the thrill of seeing history up close, the feeling of being part of something big." Searching back through the many years, it is obvious that contradictions were the norm. How could I have felt we were a vital part of a gigantic enterprise when we were not privy to very much of what was happening? Thoroughly immersed in the world's greatest drama, we never could see what effect, if any, our efforts produced.

In a writing course, the instructor challenged me. When asked what I was writing, I had replied that I was writing about my experiences during World War II. He had said, "So what's your angle? How is what you have to say any different from all the many books that are already in print?" As I continued reading the many books concerning that period, what I concluded was that they are mostly what I would call statistics. They seldom speak of what the individual soldier endured day after day, therefore lacking the personal feelings. Concentration on major battles with numbers of dead, wounded, and missing in action, of downed planes and sunken ships, omits all the mundane happenings that comprise real Army life in war. Sleeping in a foxhole under a pup tent, with one Army blanket spread on the ground, brushing away the mosquitoes, the dirt at the head sifting down into your hair and the rain water creeping in at your feet; no water to wash your dirty, smelly clothes; athletes foot stinging and itching in crusty socks; slow-healing sores from insect stings; straining to see throughout a dark night on guard duty; and days with nothing to eat—these are the true images of war. The phys-

1

ical exertions, the emotional stress, and the mental strains make up the day-to-day experiences of tension, fatigue, laughter, sorrow, and pain. The small happenings are clearly more real.

This is just a naïve attempt to tell what wartime life was like for one individual, adding the smaller missing parts to the total picture. There is so much more than statistics concerning strategy, troop movements, clashes, or generals and admirals.

The popular conception of war, the romantic picture of the running soldier with rifle in hand, is not the whole story. We were radar operators. As with any big enterprise, each man has a designated function. Our responsibility was to give early warning of enemy aircraft activity. A very portable unit, we moved quickly and frequently quite often at the front lines, close to the enemy's position.

But like most of the men in service during World War II, we were citizen-soldiers. We were equipped and trained and sent into action, but we never thought of ourselves as soldiers or part of an army. In our thinking, it was just a time-out. We had a job to do and as soon as it was finished, we were determined to get back to start our lives.

The memories of what we experienced even time cannot diminish. Some of those scattered pictures in the mind can never be erased. Unpleasant happenings we try to forget—it's proper to put them out of mind and move on. But what we forget, we are too often condemned to repeat. War, even with all its horror and suffering, or more appropriately because of those horrors, must not be forgotten.

I have tried to tell it just as we lived it, just as we felt it, even as I shake and choke up living it over again. Emotions of frustration, discouragement, and depression we all have at different times in life, but in war they run to the extreme. Yet, in spite of all else, we never felt that we were abandoned, for faith and hope were always strong.

Those who criticize the use of the atomic bomb were not there. The Japs were fanatics, they would have met us on the beaches of the Japanese homeland and the war would have dragged on with more loss of lives on both sides. If there is blame for dropping the bomb, it does not lie with those who created and used it, but with those who made it necessary. Experience showed the willingness of the Japanese to fight to the death. It had been that way throughout the Pacific War, inch by inch and day after day, across each island until all Japs were killed or captured. Critics argue that Japan was already defeated so it was not necessary to use the bomb. Actually they were beaten a year before that, but in spite of the many opportunities to surrender, the fanatics in power were dedicated to fight to the death. The mindset of those in power dictated death was preferable to the humiliation of surrender, regardless of the carnage of their own people. Conquest of Japan by conventional means would have been a massacre. American losses alone were estimated to run to 500,000.

We must never forget the sneak attack on Pearl Harbor while we were at peace. And we must not forget the cruel treatment during the Bataan death march, nor forget the torture and massacre of Allied prisoners-of-war and the atrocities perpetrated on innocent civilians in concentration camps and in native villages. Statistics show the fanaticism and disregard for human life by the Japanese; of the Allies in German prisons, 4 percent to 11 percent died while in captivity, whereas 29 percent to 40 percent of those in Japanese prisons died while prisoners. Yet unlike the Germans, the Japanese have never apologized nor admitted wrong. Walter Lippmann said, "War will never be abolished by people who are ignorant of war."

Memories—these are my scattered pictures of war.

Author—Harrison E. Lemont

Chapter 1

Preparation for War

The possibility of war, because of the crisis in Europe, filled the news in the papers and on the radio. Those daily events were a major part of our high school social studies class. I was intrigued by what was happening over there, but it never occurred to me, at the time, that it would ever involve me.

With Hitler's rise to power in Germany, he violated the surrender terms following World War I by building up the German army. In 1939 German troops moved into Austria, annexing that country. Many nations of the world protested Hitler's actions, but no country was militarily prepared to oppose him. Next Hitler began making threatening overtures toward Czechoslovakia, laying claim to some of its territory. Prime Minister Neville Chamberlain of Great Britain flew to Germany for a conference with Hitler, whereby some areas of Czechoslovakia were ceded to Germany. He returned declaring, "Peace in our time." To a high school student, these European events were fascinating.

When Germany and Russia invaded Poland, World War II began, since Britain and France were committed to go to the aid of Poland.

Nothing changed in my life. There were still school classes, basketball games, and my daily newspaper deliveries. In my senior year my schedule included all the subjects I would need for entry into college.

On December 7, 1941, as President Roosevelt called it, "a day that will live in infamy," the Japanese bombed Pearl Harbor, plunging our country into the on-going war. All men between the ages of eighteen and forty had to register with the draft board.

Now America had to gear up for an all-out war. The average citizen was completely unaware of how great the destruction was at Pearl Harbor and how ill-prepared the country actually was to fight a war. All major manufacturing industries shifted from civilian production to military needs—tanks, planes, uniforms, ammunition, and more. Every shipbuilding facility turned to the construction of ships for the navy. Everything was rationed, from butter to gasoline. Rail transportation was greatly increased. Air raid wardens—civilian volunteers—walked the streets at night to make sure no light was showing. Women were doing jobs that had heretofore only been performed by men. With the whole country involved, either in the service or war production, the many long years of the depression were over.

I still didn't realize that all this action would affect me, for wars are fought by armies. I would be graduating next spring and then on to Bates College in the fall. However, having reached eighteen and registered with the local draft board, I knew that it was just a matter of time until I would become more than just an interested bystander.

The only choice of service in those years was army or navy (which included Marines). If a man preferred the navy, he had to volunteer before he was drafted. My older brother did just that, opting for the navy. As I am very susceptible to motion sickness, the navy was not for me. I chose to wait for my call to the US Army.

It seemed that I had only begun college life, though, when all the talk was about how soon we might be called up. It was a very unsettling atmosphere, making it difficult to concentrate on one's studies. From my dorm window that fall, I watched the workmen raking the autumn leaves onto a big tarp, which they then hauled off. Having missed the first week of classes due to an infection, I was doing poorly in all my courses, in spite of studying hard on the weekends in a desperate attempt to catch up. In December I got the call from the draft board, as so many others did, to report for a physical and induction in January. To me, in one sense, it was a relief to finally know where I was going. It was late in the day when I left Bates College. The ground was covered with a new-fallen snow, and as I walked away, I looked back on the campus. The moon was sending dark shadows from the tall pines across the soft white expanse. That picture stayed clear in my mind, unfading, throughout those war years. I would return.

"Raise your right hand and repeat after me, but after 'I', insert your own name." It was a cold January day in Portland in 1943. We draftees had spent the whole day with physical and mental exams and were now being inducted into the United States Army.

One of the first things a new recruit learns concerning military life, is that there would never again be such a thing as modesty. In one big room, we were instructed to remove all our clothing. Some guys kept some of their clothing on, but when the sergeant returned and with a loud voice repeated, "All your clothing!" we stood naked and shivering, awaiting our turn to proceed down the line from one doctor to another. No part of the body was spared. We were poked and prodded with their cold metal instruments, leaving no part of the anatomy untouched. There was even the round peg and square hole mental test. As far as I could tell, we all passed. Throughout the whole day, I had been concerned that they might reject me for one reason or another; perhaps my eyesight or my head cold might be cause to leave me behind. Though the newspapers referred to "our boys in the service," no one in the army ever used that word, "boy." Henceforth we were *men*. This was mobilization of naïve, innocent youth, drafted for the duration. Regardless of what lay ahead, our lives would forever be changed.

One week was all we were allowed to get all our personal affairs in order and then board the train for Ft. Devens, Ayer, Massachusetts.

This was the beginning of a new and very different life—a time that, for me, lasted exactly three years. But because of all we endured in those years, that time has consumed a disproportionate period in my life.

We learned early about hurry up and wait, about lines, and those two letters, GI

(Government Issue). Everything became GI; even we two-legged animals were now GI's.

At Ft. Devens, to use their term, we were processed. The first step in this master plan was the issuing of the uniform. We walked in line beside a long counter through a big warehouse. At each step, we were measured—waist and leg. Those measurements were then called out to a runner who brought the pants—two pair. The whole procedure went that way with extreme efficiency—measured, the findings called out, followed by the runner with each item of clothing. All the clothing was that olive drab color, even to the shorts and handkerchiefs. Among the many items issued to us, one thing was not that drab color, but pure white—a mattress cover. We assumed that its use would become clear in time. It did! He said, "It's to bury you in! What'd you expect, a mahogany chest with brass handles?" My mattress cover, or casket, went into the bottom of my new duffel bag. Eventually it did have its use in the Philippines to enclose me, but not in the same manner the army intended. By slitting it open, it assumed the role of sheets, giving me some comfort from my scratchy army blanket.

The first afternoon of our short stay at Devens was taken up with immunization shots. We walked down a line flanked by tables loaded with bottles, cotton, and needles, administered by men in white coats. One medic grabbed my left arm and stuck me all in one smooth motion. As I turned to look at him, another fellow grabbed my right arm. Stabbed again! When I turned to him, a guy on my left again poked me many times with his small needle. "Smallpox," he said. "I've already been vaccinated for smallpox—see that scar?" This army efficiency didn't miss a beat as our line of new recruits kept moving right along.

Another shocker was the option of purchasing life insurance, another subtle suggestion that we might need that mattress cover.

Somewhere in all the hurried processing, we received our dog tags. My tag contained my name, my heir (my mother), her address, my service number, blood type O, and a "P" for Protestant religion. "You will wear them at all times and memorize that number." In all my time in the army, I obediently did as I was told, not caring to suffer the threatened consequences. Our civilian clothing and other items that might connect us with our past life were shipped home, severing any ties to freedom and emphasizing in a more dramatic fashion that we now belonged to the US Army exclusively.

All this processing was accomplished in just two days.

At night on that second day at Devens, we were put on a train with dark curtains covering the windows to avoid showing any light and sent on our way. Some guy peeking under the window covering spread the word that we were in New York and headed south. We reached our destination on a very dark night in late January and were marched from the railroad station, down a street, and right up onto a boardwalk, where we could smell and feel the ocean breeze. Most of us had no idea where we were, but some of the men knew—Atlantic City, New Jersey.

We spent one month in Atlantic City. All of the big hotels had become an army base. The rooms were converted to bunk beds with eight men to a room. The big dining rooms became mess halls. Each day we were marched out to a drill field for close order drill and calisthenics. It was a long march out to the drill area where every day was the same—nonstop physical exertion until day's end, when we fell exhausted to bed.

A couple of nights I could hear someone crying. We were all so young. My time in the Boy Scouts, off to camp for two to six weeks at a time, was a big help for me in adjusting to army life. Some of those young boys had never been away from home before.

Two days of the time spent in Atlantic City were set aside for a battery of tests—testing manual dexterity, various skills, and general knowledge. This, we were told, was to determine in what capacity we best qualified. I figured this would show me clearly the direction for my life when the war was over. But all I got from the testing was that I would be assigned to the air corps. However those of us who were picked for this branch were pleased as the US Army Air Corps was considered to be the best.

While we went through our grueling days of exertion, our preparation for war, the fighting continued on both sides of the world. The American troops were advancing across the north coast of Africa, approaching Tunisia. The Russians had triumphed at Stalingrad and were slowly pushing the Germans back. In the Pacific, after five months of fighting on Guadalcanal, by January it was secure in American hands. By the eighteenth of May, MacArthur's forces had captured the Admiralty Islands and were slowly advancing in New Guinea. In March, the Japs were driven from the Aleutian Islands of Kiska and Attu, which they had occupied for nine months.

We draftees were on the move again and it was another case of wondering where our train was taking us. Pulling into the station, we eagerly crowded the windows, anxious to see, but not until we climbed down from the train with our heavy duffel bags could we see the sign—GREENSBORO, NORTH CAROLINA.

The whole camp was under construction. The wooden barracks were just shells, with only a few of them ready for occupancy. Our group, along with another one from the South, was the first to arrive. At times there was friction between the groups, especially when the southern boys got together to sing their mournful songs that had no appeal for us Northerners. One particular tune, "No Letter in the Mail Today," I found at the time to be most irritating as they sang it over and over. But after leaving North Carolina, it sort of stuck with me and even now, singing the few lines that I can still remember can carry me back. Time tends to ease feelings and alter meanings.

For us this was more basic training—the same ritual of marching out to a drill field and then more marching and close order drill. But we were getting quite good at it. However there was one small section of the field with a patch of wild onions and every time we came to that area, as we marched around, it would bring tears to our eyes. After a few days, we had trampled it down so much that it cease to be an irritant.

After six weeks in North Carolina, it was on a train again, this time to Tampa, Florida. Though the main base was Tampa, I was constantly being sent to different bases—Bradenton, Sarasota, Venice, and Orlando in Florida; DeRitter, Louisiana; and Hattisburg and Gulfport, Mississippi. In Bradenton our tents were on a baseball field where a major league team had trained in other winter months.

Life in the South at that time was so different from New England. In the stores where they had drinking fountains, there were always two—one for whites and one for coloreds. It shocked me to find that segregation was still very much alive in the South. While at home on furlough, I couldn't walk anywhere without some driver offering me a ride. In the South, while hitching a ride to town, the only vehicles that would stop to give a soldier a ride were military vehicles.

On maneuvers in Louisiana, while crossing a field, an old man came out on his porch with a shotgun, hollering, "Get out of here, you damn Yankees!" To us, it became a standing joke as one of the guys in our platoon was actually from Louisiana.

We closely followed the news of the war. In July the Americans had landed on the island of Sicily and in September they were on the Italian mainland. In the Pacific the Gilbert and Marshall Islands (Kwajalean and Eniwetok) had been re-taken. The war was slowly but steadily turning in our favor.

Much of our time was now spent on maneuvers in areas where we had to set up our tents, practice rifle fire, and do a lot of hiking. During a time in the Florida wilderness our group was sent out to reconnoiter the area. The plan was for us to spread out in a line just far enough apart so that we could see through the dense growth to the guy on our left. I had the far right position in the formation. I had to watch where I was walking and then constantly check to keep the guy to my left in sight. Suddenly that man was gone. He had realized that he had been watching me instead of the one to his left and so he turned and raced over to where he was supposed to be. I kept going on, figuring I'd just bear to my left and eventually meet up with them. Unfortunately, as I went further, I kept coming to a multitude of small streams, preventing me from joining up with the rest of the company. I stood still and listened, trying to hear the others. But with the soft cushion of accumulated rotting matter that covered the ground, I couldn't even hear my own footsteps. I was lost! I knew if I went in a straight line, I would inevitably find some habitation, but the woods were so thick that it was difficult to get a bearing on the sun. I felt so alone that I could believe I was the first man to ever venture into this still area. Never have I experienced such quiet—no animal or bird sounds whatsoever! Even the many streams that flowed by were hushed. I could hear nothing until a couple of wild pigs appeared that at first seemed threatening, but scampered when I yelled at them.

The many small streams that coursed throughout the area blocked my every attempt at going in a straight line. By now, I was so turned around that I wasn't sure in which direction camp lay. For a while I just stood, trying to decide what to do. The streams were too wide to jump over, although they appeared to be fairly shallow. I figured if I could tie some sticks together, maybe I could cross, but I had nothing with which to tie them together and it would take hours to gather enough sticks to hold me. All I had with me was my rifle. Already two hours had passed since we left our bivouac area, earlier that morning. I thought I knew, but I wasn't sure, in which direction to head, but in any event, I had to cross those small streams. It looked like my only recourse was to wade right across each stream and head out in a straight line. They didn't look very deep, but with my first step into the water I began sinking, and the more I struggled to move, the more I kept sinking. Startled, I realized that I was in quicksand! Instinctively I threw my rifle over my head up on the land and grabbed for the branch of an overhanging bush and held on. By the time I quit sinking, I was up to my armpits. Slowly I managed to pull myself out. One stinking, dirty mess, I sat on the bank wondering what now. Surely there'd be a search party out looking for me.

Now four hours had elapsed since we first started out. I didn't know where I was, and I had no idea in which direction to go. All around me were trees and water. I had completely run out of ideas when a miracle occurred—I heard the rifles firing from camp. Everything had been so silent but now the firing practice began. It took another two hours of following the sound for me to eventually reach the path that led back to camp.

8

Getting lost wasn't entirely my fault, but the commanding officer didn't give me a chance to say anything. As he kept raving at me, questioning my fitness to ever become a real soldier, I was thinking maybe he was right. I had done fairly well to this point, though. During basic training, I wasn't one of the out-of-shape guys who was taken to the side lines during calisthenics. The obstacle courses weren't the obstacle for me that they were for some. And with close order drill, I knew my left from my right. However there was that one time when I got royally chewed out. The drill instructor had us stand at attention in formation. "You'll stand there, eyes front. You will not move a muscle. You're not to even blink until I give the order, 'at ease'." All was quiet. I kept looking straight ahead, doing just as he said. Time passed, and still no sound. I didn't know where he went. All I could see was what was dead ahead of me. It was such a long time that I was beginning to think he'd gone off and forgotten about us. I didn't move anything but my eyes to one side and there he was, right there, right beside me. I'm sure I lost some of my hearing from all his hollering.

No one liked the maneuvers, but it wasn't boring and far less restrictive than life on the base. We were trucked out in small groups, one time, to an uninhabited area of Florida, each group to a different location. Our food and equipment were to follow later on another truck. This area, with many small pines and sandy soil, was typical Florida. Apparently through some mix-up, the truck driver with our equipment didn't show up and when it began to rain, there was no cover anywhere. For a time we stood with our backs against our own small tree, which provided scant cover, as the water soaked us. Finally with no let up and being completely soaked, we built a big fire, lay down on the wet ground, and alternated drying our front and back while we slept.

There was one instance during my training, though, when I really felt good about my abilities and thoroughly impressed the officers in charge. We were taken down to a river where there were several rowboats. Each man was to get in a boat, turn it around, row across the river, and then row back. Some of the guys had obviously never been in a rowboat before. They floundered around, couldn't get the boat to turn, and dropped their oars in the water. When my turn came, I jumped into the boat and with one quick movement of the oars, one forward and the other back, turned the boat around smoothly, rowed across, reversed direction, and returned to the starting bank. While I was maneuvering so nicely, several boats were stranded and struggling in the middle of the river. Being from Maine and living on the coast, I had one big advantage.

When I got a second furlough only five months after the first one, we knew something was up. While I was at home, the news media reported that the Allies had crossed the English Channel. It was D-day, June 6, 1944. Suddenly my furlough was not all that enjoyable. I couldn't stop thinking of my friends, what was the outfit doing, and what lay ahead for us. I had to get back to Tampa. I knew we would be leaving very soon for overseas and I didn't want the war to end before I even left the United States.

Chapter 11

Territory of Hawaii

When a warrior is disabled, what matter the cause if he is unable to still function? Even the simplest thing can immobilize a person—germ-carrying mosquitoes, strained nerves, or something as simple as athlete's foot or seasickness. Seasickness is considered a joke. It's laughable to see some poor guy leaning over the railing, throwing up. But to the fellow who is turning green while he spews his guts out, there's nothing funny about it.

As a child, I had always been very susceptible to motion sickness. On a trip from Connecticut to California, my father fumed about having had to stop five times so I could throw up even before we had reached the city limits. "How are ever going to get to California?" he said with a voice that increased several decibels. But with a minor adjustment, we were on our way again. I held in my lap my baby brother's one-handled, white porcelain potty, so I could throw up and my father could continue driving.

What I had heard concerning life on a rolling ocean had much to do with my choice of service, army or navy. The navy had been my father's career and my older brother, Bob, following in his footsteps, was already on a ship somewhere between New London, Connecticut, and Brazil. No rocking boat for me, I needed solid ground, so it would be the only other option, the army. Unfortunately as I headed for war, it was going to be across water—by ship, by rolling, rocking, bobbing, stomach-churning ship.

When I hurriedly returned to camp after my furlough, the whole company was full of rumors and speculation. "If we're going to Europe, we'll get light clothing. It's cold there but they like to confuse enemy spies. If it's to the Pacific, where it's hot, they'll give us woolens. That'll be the tip-off." And so the rumors went.

We packed all our possessions in our duffel bags and boarded the train. When we left Tampa, Florida, as usual we didn't know where we were headed. It turned out to be a six-day train trip from Tampa to Seattle. Under different circumstances it might have been an enjoyable adventure, seeing so much of America, if only we could have stopped where and when we chose. It seemed almost intended that we have a good look at the country for which we would be fighting. As the train went through Macon and Atlanta, Georgia, and then over to

Birmingham, Alabama, and then north, we concluded that it was not Europe but the Pacific for us. During the night we went through Tennessee and Kentucky and awoke in Illinois. When we reached the Mississippi River, our train halted right on the bridge. Up to this point it had been a rather steady, non-stop, day and night ride, watching the differing scenery pass by the window. It was a fortuitous stroke of luck that we stopped right over the Mississippi River so that we had time to admire America's dividing line, the father of waters. While we waited for other train traffic to clear, we watched the many different boats maneuvering the river.

From Missouri it was north through Iowa, where all along the way people would be waving to us and when we stopped, they'd give us magazines or newspapers. At one railroad station they gave us coffee and doughnuts.

Days and nights passed as we traveled north into Minnesota. We could walk around on the train or sit and talk or read. Some guys got a group together to play cards. All our meals were cold as there was no dining car on a troop train. With no stops, just the steady rumbling of the train wheels, it was west through North Dakota where the gently rolling, treeless hills were covered with wavy green that looked like a vast open sea. We citizen-soldiers had become so conditioned to doing whatever we were told, that we had become complacent, even lacking concern or speculation about our future. We just had an urge to get this job done so we could start living. In Montana, where we halted at a small railroad station, we descended from the train for calisthenics. It was always good to be off the train for a break. As far as one could see, except for the small railroad station, there was nothing to see just gently rolling, flowing hills in every direction. Before we returned to the train, we did see a fellow on a horse come over one hill and head for the railroad station.

Crossing Washington State, the railroad tracks followed the rivers that cut deeply into the mountains. Sometimes the tracks were on one side of the river and then they would cross over to continue along the other bank, occasionally passing through a tunnel in a mountain.

Arriving in Seattle late on the seventh of July, we went straight to Ft. Lawton, where we spent three days with preparation exercises and instructions. We turned in our worn-out uniforms for new. We had rifle and gas mask checks; lectures on bonds, censorship, and personal affairs; and a fire drill. We practiced abandoning ship by climbing up and down a wooden wall on a rope netting. In the evenings we did have some free time for a movie or a visit to the PX. In those years, there was still segregation in the service. One night at the PX there was a confrontation between some white and black soldiers. I never found out what started it or how it ended. I just slipped out a side door. It struck me as a sad beginning to what we all had ahead—petty differences between men who were committed to fight the nation's enemy, not each other.

With preliminaries over, we boarded a "Banana Boat," the *SS Mexico*, a ship converted to troop transport from its former use as a merchant vessel bringing fruit from the Caribbean to the US.

In addition to our men, in another part of the *SS Mexico* was a group of Italian POWs being taken to Hawaii to work in the fields. These POWs were convinced by their own propaganda that Hawaii was a war zone. Before they boarded the ship, there was an uprising that was quickly quelled by the MPs. After we docked in Honolulu Harbor, they were the first to be taken off the ship, so we got a chance to see the compartment where they had been lodged. They had written all over the walls, "The PW will not forget", condemning the US for this violation of the Geneva Convention. They had painted crossed German and Italian flags and written some messages in Italian.

After we boarded the ship and stowed our gear, I braced for the anticipated sickness, but after an hour on the ship, there was no feeling of nausea. I was quite pleased with myself until someone told me that we were still tied to the dock. The next day, though, that dreaded time came. We moved out from shore and yet I still felt okay—either nothing like carsickness or maybe I had outgrown it. What I didn't realize was that Puget Sound can be very calm. After we left the confines of the Sound and reached the Pacific Ocean, as the boat dipped down, my breakfast came up, and so did my lunch and supper and the next day and the next. It was a seven-day agonizing trip to Hawaii. I was so miserable that I would have welcomed a Japanese torpedo. The deck beneath my feet was constantly moving. No wonder sailors walk so funny. After days of vomiting, I figured I had to do something about it. Maybe the ship's doctor could give me something. I stood in the long sick-call line to get to see him, but I kept losing my place in line while I ran to the railing one more time.

One cannot go indefinitely without food. For a time I felt calmed while waiting in the chow line, but when the line reached the steps that led down to the mess hall and the steamy odor of food came up and hit me, I had to leave. Military chow looks like regular food until the auto mechanic-turned-cook works on it. It's barely palatable if one is feeling well. Especially upsetting are the green beans that are subjected to a hunk of fat while they die in the cooking.

From early morning to dark, I held my place on deck, not daring to leave the rail. The rest of the company left me to my misery. Regardless of how I felt, I still had to take my routine place on the duty roster—KP, carrying stores, and taking food to the Italian prisoners.

Sickness of any kind, I rationalized, can be a case of mind over matter. The ship's intercom had announced the showing of a movie in one of the wardrooms, which sounded like the psychological diversion I needed. I could lose myself in some other thoughts and forget about the second-hand meal I had just dropped to the fish. Unfortunately, just as I stepped into the room, the movie was *Mutiny on the Bounty*, and the picture on the screen at that very moment was of the three-masted ship, *HMS Bounty*, rocking in a big storm. That's all I saw of that movie.

The army officials checked us routinely for venereal disease and issued snake-bite kits, gas masks, and water purification tablets, none of which were ever of use to me. No mention was ever made of seasickness, how to cope with it or how to prevent it.

A few days before we reached Hawaii, I began to adjust to a life on a rolling platform. When we disembarked from that horrid, stomach-wrenching ship that brought us to Honolulu Harbor, that dock sure felt solid and steady under foot.

Though the Territory of Hawaii was part of the United States, we felt we were in a foreign country. The people wore different clothing and the names on the street signs we saw, as our truck carried us through the city on our way to Camp Bellows, were unpronounceable.

At Camp Bellows our tents were pitched right on a sandy beach. The clear, refreshing, warm water and the many opportunities we had to avail ourselves of it was not our idea of war. Swimming every day in the beautiful surf was great until the day I came into contact with a Portuguese man-of-war. The jellyfish back home were just that—a lump of jelly and perfectly harmless. This thing left a swelling ridge all along my arm with a stinging like a thou-

Berard Gross and Harrison E. Lemont

sand bees. It was a while before I went in swimming again, which was done very timidly. I never wanted to mess with his kind again.

The weather in Hawaii was hotter than in Florida, but with an ever-present ocean breeze. Because of the hot nights, we slept in just our briefs. We covered our cots with mosquito netting to ward off flying insects and put lime on and around the legs of the cot to stop the crawling ones.

Our next camp location was down a road, through a sugar cane field, to the top of a rise, right next to a big pineapple field. I didn't really care that much for pineapple. Cutting them up, all that sticky juice, and having to eat it with our hands was a mess. It was a fifty dollar fine if we were caught picking pineapples, so we had to keep the tent flaps closed. But the fruit was right there and we were young, and risk added to the enjoyment of our pineapple.

Our time in Hawaii may have been a peaceful time, but it wasn't restful. We were commandeered to be longshoremen, spending many days on the docks, working some nights until five in the morning unloading ships. I don't believe that was in my job description. It may have been, though, as I do not recall seeing a copy of what I signed up to do.

One of our days was spent on a practice maneuver; and as it turned out, we all, navy included, did need practice.

Early in the morning, we boarded a large transport ship in the harbor and headed for an isolated area of another island. Equipment and small craft had already been loaded. One of the navy's tasks during this drill was to hoist one of the big army tanks from the ship's deck and lower it into a waiting landing craft below. However, and fortunately for the small craft, before it was in place beside the ship, the chains attached to the tank slipped or broke and the tank was last seen as it plunged beneath the surface of the water. No wonder wars cost so much! That multi-million dollar machine never got a chance to fire its guns or disrupt enemy activities.

Loaded down with gear, we scrambled down the net on the side of the ship and into the waiting LCVP (landing craft vehicle personnel) where each boat then circled in the rolling surf until all were launched and loaded so we could charge to the beach together. Round and round we went, bobbing in the ocean swells while some men, myself included, were throwing up. When all the small boats were ready, we finally raced to shore. I staggered up the beach with my machine gun across my arms, wishing it was not just practice and some sharpshooter would end my misery. It's not clear what was learned by that day of practice. As for me, I was so seasick that, next time, if I had a choice I was going to swim to shore.

Our time spent in Hawaii, though varied, was a restless period. We were anxious to get on with our mission.

The war in Europe didn't hold our attention much now that we knew we were headed in the other direction. The various towns, rivers, and bridge names in the daily news didn't mean much to us anyway. In the Pacific war, the Americans had landed on Saipan in the Marianas, in our steady island-hopping advance.

Finally we got the hoped-for pass to get to see this fabled land, Honolulu and also Wakiki Beach. From camp by trolley bus we headed for Wakiki. Maybe some of the let-down was due to all the hype and the build-up of anticipation, but that famous beach didn't look as big as the one in my hometown.

In Honolulu the army and navy men considerably out-numbered the local inhabitants.

The city was what is termed "wide open." It was not difficult, if one chose, to locate one of the many houses of pleasure. Just look for the sign above the door or the uniformed men waiting in line. Store windows displayed cards and pictures of naked women in many poses, all of which were for sale inside the store. Some time later, the city officials were pressured into making some changes, so pictures were no longer allowed in the store windows and the signs above the ladies' houses were removed.

In the city there wasn't much that we could buy since we were low on funds and there was little for sale of interest to us anyway. I would have liked a Hershey bar, with or without nuts, but the candy that was for sale was what would be termed homegrown and of limited choice—coconut or pineapple.

All the money we received in bills was marked with big letters reading HAWAII. I never learned why. Nor did I ever learn why we received our pay in pesos in the Philippines or yens in Okinawa, when the only place we could use this money was at American facilities and the money was printed by the US.

Since 1944 was an election year, although it was July, we received absentee ballots so we could vote for president.

For entertainment on those many times that we were confined to the camp area, the army set up a big screen to show movies. Our seating was the sandy ground. As the show ended one night, everyone got up to head back to our tents. In the sudden commotion, one very confused and disoriented mouse, startled by the many trampling feet, ran up Gross's pants leg. His cries and jumping about brought forth hysterics on the part of the rest of us in the platoon. It sure wasn't funny for Gross, but it did take a while before we could stop laughing long enough to empathize with him. Gross did manage to trap the mouse and squeeze it until it fell dead from his pants leg, but not before it bit him.

There was so much air activity with planes constantly coming and going that we paid them little notice. However on one day when two planes collided just off our beach with a big explosion, we watched as the debris fell into the ocean and one parachute opened. To us, this impromptu air show had a very chilling effect. It gave us an eerie feeling of just what was ahead.

It was as if coconut candy bars, pictures of nude women, fresh pineapple, jelly fish, a lost army tank, and one small mouse meshed together to form a crazy pattern, a prelude to our mixed-up life to come.

Chapter III

Our War Began with Water

If I could stick my head inside a filthy, foul-smelling garbage can while my world rolled incessantly on a lurching ocean and then emerge not gagging and running to the rail, I felt I'd finally mastered the ocean. Cleaning garbage cans was one part of KP duty that we were each assigned. Though proud of myself for overcoming seasickness, I still had no desire to be a part of anyone's navy.

We spent five weeks on the great expanse of the Pacific Ocean en route to war, from Hawaii to Eniwetok to the Admiralty Islands, then to the Philippines. Our dwelling, a troop transport ship, on this leg of our journey seemed like a small floating tin can in a world of water with nothing in sight in any direction from the horizon, a circle of water surrounded us. If one did not look down at the water as our ship cut through the blue-green ocean, one could feel that the ship stood still, like a bobbing cork floating in a pail of water. The whole world was water and we were the only living humans. White puffs of clouds filled a quiet, light blue sky during the day. The sky at night was dark blue. The moon would reflect on the water, while the phosphorescence gleamed like a reflection of the many stars as the ship was enclosed in water, creating an incredibly beautiful scene, a prelude to the ugliness that was to come.

So unlike our many previous moves, which were, "pack your gear and report to a specific location," when we boarded the *USS Baxter* in Hawaii, we knew we were headed for a war zone. For the first time we were even told where we were going.

As soon as our ship hit the open sea, with no chance for word to leak out, we were gathered in a ward room and told that we would be a part of the invasion of Yap Island.

Yap is located approximately 1,000 miles on a direct line east of the Philippines. Our radar unit would be located on a hill overlooking the airstrip on Gagil-Tomil Island, just off the coast of the main Yap Island. Eagerly we studied the maps in an effort to learn whatever we could about our destination.

Yap is actually a group of twenty small islands populated by approximately 5,000 Micronesians. The Spaniards, who first discovered the islands, sold them to Germany in 1899.

After World War I, they became Japanese-mandated islands. Japan was using these islands as a naval and air base. After the war, in 1947 the islands became, by act of the United Nations, a trusteeship of the United States.

We were so accustomed to not knowing where we were going that Bensick went around saying, "I know where we are going, yap, yap, yap."

Though we grumbled about having calisthenics, it was good to keep us physically active. Because of a shortage of space, though, only twenty men could exercise for one hour each day. Exercising on a moving platform was somewhat difficult, for when we jumped up our landing place was not in the same place it was when we left it.

In the sleeping compartments, the bunks were stacked five high where the ceiling permitted. In other areas where a fuel or water pipe ran through the living quarters, the bunks along that line were only four bunks high. So close together were the bunks that in order to turn over, one had to get out and crawl back in, unless that individual had very narrow hips. Some of the time we chose to sleep on deck. But there, too, it was a choice—either we withstood the hardness of the deck or the stuffiness of the below-deck quarters. The decks were usually crowded at night so apparently others chose, as I did, to be out in the fresh air.

The temperature was so extremely hot as we neared the equator, that periodically water would be pumped onto the deck to cool down the ship. It's a wonder that ships float with everything made of metal. I acquired several bumps to the head while going up and down the gangways. The food was good and plentiful, with the cooks baking fresh bread daily. But because the mess hall was hot and stuffy and our world was constantly moving, we all experienced a general lack of appetite. We had fresh water for drinking and cooking, but our showers were salt water.

Completely unaware that the big brass had changed plans, our ship rendezvoused at Eniwetok. The US had chosen to bypass Yap, leaving it, as with many other bases to wither. Eniwetok is a circle of small islands formed by the top ring of an extinct volcano. During wartime so much is secretive. We had to wait for the history books, long after the events, to learn what was taking place at the time. It was at Eniwetok that our SAW (Signal Aircraft Warning) Company was re-assigned, from Admiral Chester Nimitz's command to General Douglas MacArthur's for the intended liberation of the Philippines. As a safe enclosure for a gathering of a multitude of ships, Eniwetok Atoll provided a vast anchorage for the navy. It became an ideal staging base for further amphibious operations in the Pacific War. In all my brief years of life, I had never seen so many ships in total, much less all in one place. The lagoon was crowded with ships of all kinds.

Eniwetok is one of many islands in the Marshall Island group, as is Kwajalean. Like Yap, the Marshall Islands were a protectorate assigned to the Japanese at the end of World War I. The Americans landed on Kwajalein on January 30, 1944. In February it took just six days for the Americans to take Eniwetok Atoll from the 3,500 Jap defenders.

Though we were allowed to go ashore for the day, there wasn't much to see. It was a much appreciated change, however, to be on solid ground, if only for a few hours. We explored some embattled defensive fortifications. The short walk from the lagoon side to the ocean side on any one of these many small chain-links, this string of beads, was only sand and palm trees. Reviewing the notes I made back then, it states, "We assembled at 1:30 to return to the ship, left for the ship at 4:00, and found our ship at 6:30." It's an indication of how big the lagoon was and the difficulty of locating one's own ship among the thousands of others. The lagoon was so large that one could not see across to the small islands on the far side even if there were no ships blocking one's view.

September 28, 1944, we left Eniwetok Atoll and were again alone in our expanse of blue water. For the next few days we did occasionally catch a glimpse of some of the other ships. Each day varied little from the previous day. As before, reading, card playing, talking, and letter writing were our salvation from boredom. Gross and I spent many hours together.

Back in the States during our training, the army was constantly moving us around, so I'm not sure when Gross and I met. We seemed to have a lot in common. When on leave, we didn't head for the bars as so many did, but were more interested in seeing the city of Tampa. One night as we passed the hospital just as two nurses were leaving the building, Gross suggested we approach them with no specific idea in mind. Being shy, especially with women, I held back while he went over to talk with them. I saw them listening politely, but from the shake of their heads, I gathered they were not interested. They obviously were unaware of the little they had to fear from these two young soldiers.

Gross taught me how to play two-handed bridge as well as chess. We would move around the ship following what shade we could find, sitting on the hard deck to read or write.

I think it was during those many days on the Pacific Ocean that Gross and I became so close that a bond was created. On many occasions no word was required between us—we knew each other so well. Gross was such an easy person to be with. He was not quite as tall as I was and had black curly hair and a demure mannerism that was misleading as to his strong personal identity. We seemed to match or complement each other. I was the daring one, while he was cautious. He seemed to temper my unbridled recklessness.

On October third, we reached Manus Island in the Admiralties, a group of islands off the north coast of New Guinea. En route we crossed the International Date Line, completely losing forever Wednesday, September 20, 1944. We went to sleep Tuesday the nineteenth and in the morning it was Thursday the twenty-first. However, on our way home after the war, we did gain a day. Manus Island was a staging area, crowded with men, sailors and soldiers from many different outfits and different countries. Such a mixture of men makes you realize the importance of the chain of command.

Gross and I went ashore on the small island of Pityilu for a swim in a pool. It was a restful time without a rolling world where we could relax. But it was a brief respite for word came for us to get back to the *Baxter* and load up our gear. Weighted down with our duffel bags, we boarded a small boat that took us to our new ship. It was a transfer from our somewhat comfortable troop transport ship to one of the newly created LSTs (Landing Ship Tank). These LSTs were designed for beaching, discharging their cargo right up on the beach. With their fairly flat bottoms, they were certainly not intended for open ocean travel. Rumor had it that they sometimes actually stood on end or rolled from side to side.

After having overcome my seasickness by learning the techniques of shipboard motion, boarding LST 704 with its reports of erratic movement had me dreading the change.

If I could stick my head in those stinking garbage cans, I felt I could meet any challenge. However, I knew in the months to come we would be called upon to make many adjustments and face many new challenges in a completely foreign environment.

Chapter IV

Living under an LCT

" You are about to take part in one of the greatest campaigns in United States history: the campaign to free the Philippines." This was the opening line in the handbook, *To the Philippines*, just one of the many items we were issued as we left the Admiralty Islands on an LST (Landing Ship Tank). The LST was a ship with big doors and a ramp in the bow, designed specifically for the shallow-grade beaches in that amphibious warfare. It became our home on the last leg of our journey en route to war.

The LST (Landing Ship Tank) was originally intended for short hauls from port of embarkation to the beach. It had been employed extensively in the crossing of the English Channel in the invasion of Normandy, France, the previous June. During those war years sixty different types of landing craft were built in the US, with major and minor landing craft totaling over 46,000. More than fifteen hundred LSTs were built.

On this type of ship there are quarters only for the sailors manning the ship. Our accommodations on LST 704 were on the ship's deck. Fastened securely, we hoped, and set up on blocks was an LCT (Landing Craft Tank) being piggybacked on our ship. Because this LCT consumed most of the deck, our sleeping area was under it. This type of landing craft was made to carry six medium tanks. Although it was designed to charge right up onto the beach, it was still not completely flat. The center portion was only about four feet from the LST's deck, while headroom at the sides was about six feet. We had our cots lined up in rows under it. The guys in the middle of the pack had very little headroom. Because of my aversion to tight places, I chose to have the outermost cot. I rather doubt if I would have had much rest lodged in such a tight enclosure. Then, too, I was not completely sure that our covering would stay in place as our ship rolled with the ocean's swells. Unfortunately, though, I was the one most exposed to the elements, being on the outer fringe. It became routine each morning for me to spread my blankets and clothing items out to let the hot tropical sun dry them off.

It wasn't long after our ship departed Manus Island, which is located just north of New Guinea, that we were assembled for the briefing on our destination. Among the additional items we received were ration packets and a snake-bite kit. The handbook, *To the Philippines*, was a very informative little booklet with chapters including, "Why We Are Going into the

Philippines." It was filled with facts about the people, the history, the terrain, cities, islands, and language. The booklet ended with, "All your military experience since you first got into uniform has been leading up to this, the invasion of the Philippines." Before this move there had been the battle for Guadalcanal in the Solomon Islands, and the slow torturous fight along the north coast of New Guinea. Finally General MacArthur was poised for the return to the Philippine Islands and we became part of that liberation. The pamphlet's introduction ends with a statement reading this was "the last stretch." As it turned out, at least for us, it was not an ending, but only a beginning.

During the long monotonous days at sea, it was pleasant sitting on my cot watching the ocean waves, the white caps breaking the otherwise calm water. I could write letters or join in on a card game. It had been rumored that on the open ocean, the LSTs would sometimes stand on end or rock from side to side but that erratic movement did not materialize. It was actually a rather calm and pleasant trip. Leaning on the rail at night I could watch the sun sink into the ocean, sending forth red lightning which seemed to set the sky on fire.

However, my daily routine was upset one day when I appeared at the medic's door with blood dripping from my finger. Among those many items that we had been issued in preparation for our landing was soap, and not picturesquely wrapped, aromatically scented cleansing bars. This was big chunks of brown, slippery stuff, guaranteed to kill any germ and most anything else with which it came into contact. It also was deemed suitable for washing clothes. In order to put that soap into a form that would make it more usable, it had to be cut into sizes that could be more easily carried and stored.

Would that man were gifted with foresight, for if so, I never would have sharpened my knife, at least not to such a razor-sharp edge; and, too, I would have known that the knife would go through that stuff like that often quoted hot-knife-and-butter simile. But who else would have been so stupid as to hold it in his hand while cutting it anyway? I didn't push the knife all that hard, or at least I didn't think I had but it went right through the soap and across my index finger, cutting it open to where I could see the cord was also severed, although not completely through.

No doctor was assigned duty on this small landing craft, only a medic. When I had appeared at the medic's doorway with my bleeding finger, the look on his face said more than I wanted to hear. He obviously knew about Band-Aids for a scratch, but this clearly said "stitch" and for that he was very apprehensive. I completely lost my confidence in him when it was clear that he was not sure as he thumbed through his medical books where to find the proper instructions. When he finally found his page, his confidence was restored, but mine was not. Then he assumed a very professional air, spraying the cut with a freezing gunk, alcoholing the needle, and threading the needle. This was the point at which I figured I'd better sit down. He brought the needle to my bleeding finger and poked it in one side, across the opening and over to the other side. "Just like sewing up the Thanksgiving turkey," he said. However, his moment of triumph was short-lived since he hadn't secured the end of the thread and the whole thing went right through the skin. So he had to start over, but at least that next time he already had the needle holes.

All the while he was working on his sewing, my greatest concern was whether this would heal so he could remove his lovely embroidery before we had to leave the ship, and if not, then what?

I've often wondered if that medic ever got a chance to use his new found skill on someone else and just maybe this brief incident had a positive purpose.

Fortunately, later on, when I returned to see the medic again, he found the cut had healed enough so he could remove the stitches. He replaced the bandage with what he was well experienced with—a Band-Aid.

Gross's bunk was next to mine and on those long sunny days we spent many hours in small talk. Some days others—Finnigan, Dymond, Odell, Bensick—would join us for a game of pinochle.

As the end of our journey drew near, with only a couple of days until landing, I went below deck to see about our equipment. I wanted to be certain that all was ready. It was at that time that I was exposed to one of life's many lessons. That's where I found Stone. I had first met Stone back in the States when I was transferred into the outfit he was in, the 555th SAW Co. At that time he was a sergeant, broken to private the next day, but at the time very much in command. He was not very tall, maybe five-feet-eight or nine inches and stout, but displaying physical strength. Stone never walked, he swaggered. I never knew anyone who oozed such self-confidence, who was so sure of himself. He never overlooked an opportunity to let anyone who would listen know how great he was. Stone was tattooed from neck to waist and if you were to express interest, he would gladly tell you about each and every one of those needlepoint pictures. He was macho, poised, and bragged constantly, never hesitating to enlighten any listener of his previous night's conquest. In that crotch area of the body, he was very well endowed. Of course, that is not the way he described it, but as he said, none of the women he was acquainted with ever refused him.

With Stone, I think I envied his self-satisfied, secure bearing. In the military service, one gets to know another very quickly, and you tend to spend most of your time with the ones who are more of your thinking. But each one becomes a part of your family. You accept each other with or without faults. That's how it was with Stone and me; I understood him, I thought I knew him, and as with all the others, we were one in spirit. Stone went from sergeant to private, to corporal, to sergeant, and back to private. It seemed to go with how much he drank the night before or how well he controlled his mouth or how late he was to formation. But no matter, being broken in rank somehow amounted to an accomplishment with Stone. Though we traveled in different circles, within the unit we were still one.

Below deck that day, I had found Stone sitting on the floor, crouched in a corner, his back to the wall, trembling. This macho, strutting, bragging guy was literally frightened to death. He grabbed my arm in a pleading manner, rambling incoherently, words that made no sense to me. I think if it had happened in my later years, perhaps I might have had words of wisdom to impart, calming words of consolation, but no word of mine at that time had any effect. I could only leave him as I had found him.

After the landing, our time was consumed with consolidating our position, digging foxholes, and preparing defenses while coping with excitement, confusion, deafening noise, and utter pandemonium. So a few days passed before I saw Stone again. He was the same old Stone, still not walking but swaggering talking of everything and nothing. We spoke greetings, but said nothing of what had occurred on the ship, and I never mentioned it to him or anyone else. It was a special secret that two shared but never acknowledged.

Our relationship was just as before. The only change was the impact that revelation had within me. I could not explain my inner feelings, nor could I explain the simple delight I felt in having Stone be Stone again and my having had a glimpse of the real Stone when just for a brief time I saw beyond his macho facade.

On the morning of October 20, 1944, we were roused early as our ship was entering Leyte Gulf. All the world seemed to be exploding. The ships of battle were all firing at the island of Leyte, with planes from the carriers joining in. That water enclosure was packed with ships. Our ship maneuvered into position behind the ships of war—battleships, cruisers, destroyers.

We were instructed to fold up our gear, stow the cots, and get out of the way on the stern of the vessel. In what seemed like a machine-efficiency drill, the navy men went about the task of launching the LCT from the deck of our ship. Skids were arranged, our ship was tipped to an awkward angle, and the LCT slipped off into the water with one big splash. Our LCT would be loaded with tanks and other personnel, which were being transported by another ship for its advance to the beach. Our time was yet to come.

As we waited, we looked all about us at the action that we were privileged to watch, a sight that many would never see. History was being made and we had front row seats.

It seems that in every action in life there is at least one element that is unpredicted, even bizarre. In the water swimming around our ship were snakes. Never have I ever seen so many snakes—too many to count the number. During the briefing on the island, we had been given instructions for the use of our snake-bite kits and were told that there were many kinds of snakes in the Philippines—some harmless and others not. Yet in the following months from the landings at San Jose, over the mountains to Ormoc, and then back to the east coast of Leyte, never once did we see even one snake. Either they all drowned or they abandoned the island. It was just as well for I had long since discarded the snake-bite kit as one less thing to have to carry. It went the way of the gas mask.

During those horrendous days there was no time to admire the waving palms or the sandy beach, no time even to think, just move forward as instructed. With the deafening noise and the moving earth, there could be no hesitation. We just kept moving on into the devastation that lay before us.

Just hours after we left LST 704, it received a direct hit from one of the many Jap planes that were attacking our landing site. All the men still aboard the ship were killed.

Chapter V

Baptized in War

On the afternoon of October 20, 1944, when our ship hit the shore of the island of Leyte, the big doors of the LST swung open, the ramp dropped, and our truck, loaded with men and equipment, drove out onto the sandy beach even before the bulldozers had finished pushing sand up to the bow of the ship to create their improvised runway. By this time the area was fairly cleared of enemy troops as the infantry had done their job. In the morning, when our ship first ground to a halt on the shore, I had stood on the ship's bow, mesmerized, watching the bulldozer operators being shot off of their machines by snipers in the trees and being quickly replaced by another driver as they pushed beach sand up to the entries of the many landing ships. Men loaded down with gear were running in all directions, and many still, quiet bodies were strewn across this sandy beach.

Two days prior to this, we had been assembled in the wardroom of the ship where maps marked TOP SECRET were tacked to the walls. An officer, with pointer in hand, was indicating on his clear maps the various code names and locations where each unit would disembark. "Orange Two" was the code name for the area of the shore where our ship would beach. It was near San Jose on the east coast of Leyte. Although San Jose was indicated on a map of the island, it only consisted of a scattering of native huts.

Nothing in my early youthful years nor in the months spent in Army training could possibly have prepared me for the horror that we were about to experience.

The whole world seemed to be exploding with flashing lights in every direction coupled with constant rumbling, thundering noises. We could see the hilly land light up with each red flash.

When I was a young kid in Norfolk, Virginia, my father had taken the family to see the town's fireworks display. I was awed and a little frightened by all the noise and sparkling lights. The crowd was being constantly admonished to keep well back. Standing on the ship's deck watching this devastation triggered my memory of that forth of July celebration so long ago. But this was not a show, this was real and it was gigantic. All the bright, flaming lights were from ships of all sizes with their big guns sending explosives into the island. As I gazed

23

up and down all along the shore, the navy guns would fire and there'd be a big explosion in the interior. It was constant—no slowing of the booming noise and explosions. Japanese and American planes overhead were firing at each other. Jap planes were firing at the island and at the ships. Their bombers were releasing their bombs as they flew over, striking at the ships, and hitting the beach area. Many planes were crashing into the sea. For hours there was no ceasing. Even after we had beached, along with the many other LSTs on each side of us, the noise never abated.

Suddenly the anti-aircraft gun right beside me opened up on a Jap plane that was coming directly toward us. It shocked me out of my stupor, bringing me back to reality. There was no town policeman here telling the crowd to keep back out of danger. I realized that I was the only soldier on deck and I had better get below deck with everyone else and leave this scene to the navy gunners.

The island's beach could have been a picture-postcard scene with soft white sand stretching in each direction for as far as one could see, with tall waving coconut palms just beyond the sand. Sheltered by Leyte Gulf, the calm clear water was leisurely rolling in and out on this smooth sandy shore. It should have contained umbrellas and sunbathers in skimpy bathing suits, maybe a picnic basket or volleyball net, but not here, not now, for this was war and with the landing it was strewn with dead bodies and all the rest of war's trash. Those clear, clean maps bore little resemblance to what we saw.

It's amazing how quickly the human being can adapt to such a vastly different existence. It was a blessing that so much was happening in so little time, punctuated by commotion, confusion, and earth-shattering explosions, for it allowed no time to think or speculate.

As we moved out, our overloaded truck had in tow a small utility trailer with more of our equipment. We were making our own road as we moved out on the soft, narrow, sandy strip, when suddenly our trailer slid sideways and was caught hanging off the sand ramp, halting our movement. Stymied as we were, we had to unload the trailer and disconnect it from the truck and then physically maneuver it back onto the track. While attempting to disconnect the jammed trailer hitch, one guy had his hand mangled when it became caught in the coupling, thus ending his wartime experiences.

Our first priority once we got situated on land was to prepare our defenses. We dug individual foxholes and used our pup tents for covering. Our platoon was scattered around in a coconut palm tree area. The digging in the sandy soil was fairly easy in the scrubby grass, yet the soil was firm enough to hold in place. Though steady rain and constant gun fire continued non-stop throughout that first night, sleep was sill possible after all the day's expended energy and nervous excitement. We still had some of the K rations that had been issued to us before leaving the ship, but exhaustion gave sleep precedence over food. When I lay down, I removed my army boots, but for the first couple of weeks we never got a chance to remove any other bit of clothing. During that first night, as the rain continued, I had to keep pulling my feet up as the water at the foot of the foxhole began rising. But when I did, the sand at the top sifted down into my hair. It was just the first of many difficult nights—an introduction to our new way of life.

Before dawn the medics had removed the wounded and the burial detail had carried off the dead. In the morning mist, through noise and confusion, the natives—in a state of shock—began slowly coming down from the hills, crossing over fallen trees, blasted holes in the earth,

Landing on Leyte Island, Philippines—October 20, 1944

and scrubby brush. They were fleeing all the crashing manmade thunder that was accosting them from every direction. They were clothed mostly in rags. The little ones, with no clothing at all, were clinging to their mothers. At first they were shy and afraid, but even with the language barrier they were eager to convey to us how pleased they were that we had finally arrived. It was as if each of us individually had been expected. In the days that followed, we heard many tales of torture, killing, rape, and painful, slow death perpetrated on these helpless people by the Japs. The young Filipino children had the best command of the English language and would come to our general area to talk with us. We enjoyed seeing the kids and talking with them about their life, family, schooling, hopes, and plans. I asked one twelve-year-old boy if he could tell me who Sergio Osmena was. His quick response clearly showed that he was bright: "The vice-president of the Philippine Islands," he said. They were unaware that Osmena was now president, as President Manuel Quezon had died in the United States while heading his government in exile. Two days after our landing date, I came down with dengue fever. According to the medical books, dengue fever is endemic throughout the tropics, transmitted by the female Aedes mosquito after feeding on an infected person. Immediately after being bitten the individual may develop a fever that lasts from one to three days. Symptoms include fever, headache, and severe eye, bone, and muscle pain. Fatigue may persist for several weeks. Treatment includes non-aspirin analgesic and fluid replacement to combat dehydration due to high fever. Recommended cures included "place patient on a hypothermia blanket or administer a tepid sponge bath. Spray liberally with insect repellent." I had all those symptoms, although the aches and fever seemed like a really bad case of the flu. We had no insect repellent and my chances of having a sponge bath, tepid or otherwise, were pretty slim.

As I lay on my palm-leaf bed, pulling my blanket up and then pushing it off in tune with my fever, I heard someone say, "We're pulling out." Orders had come down from headquarters for all units to leave the beach area. We were directed to load up everyone and relocate up in the hills. All the tents and equipment were to remain in place. "Just leave me here," I said. "I'm too sick to move. I just want to be left alone." Little did I know how alone I would be. *It's just another of the many army drills that seem to have so little purpose,* I figured. *I'll just wait right here in my foxhole until they return.* As I heard the last of the trucks roll out and the stillness settle in, I realized I was the only one left. It was a long, quiet, dark night. Strangely quiet. I woke frequently, but could not hear even the sound of gunfire that we had become so accustomed to. I would listen for a while and then drift off to sleep again. At dawn everyone returned. The reason for their leaving was a mystery to me and I supposed of no importance. But it was another case of "what we do not know." Many years later I learned why the precaution of having everyone move and what might have happened. Out in the ocean off our coast a naval battle was developing that would be known as "the Battle of Leyte Gulf." All the vessels that were to protect our beachhead had been sent out to chase the Jap fleet, leaving us completely exposed to any possible enemy counterthrust.

The Japanese had planned to lure Admiral Halsey's ships away to chase a contingent of their fleet. The other Japanese ships were divided into two forces to approach Leyte from the west, one group going to the north of the island, the other to the south. Fortunately the remaining American ships blocked the two narrow entrances by sinking or dismantling the lead ships.

If the Japs had landed reinforcements behind us, I doubt if I could have held them off. Well, maybe, if I weren't so sick.

But for a few hours, this whole camp, the whole beach area, I guess even the whole war, was mine and I slept through it.

We were well conditioned to the waiting that was so much a part of army life. Delayed orders as to where we were to position our radar set and establish our camp allowed us time to scout around and see some of the area. Gross, Dymond, and I started out following a small dirt road that led inland. The weather in the Philippines doesn't seem to vary. Each day is as hot as the day before. On this day we got our first view of what the tropical sun does to a dead human body left exposed in the hot, humid climate. He had apparently died in a sitting position, for his body was rigid in an awkward pose. The corpse was blue in color and the bloating was straining against what clothing still clung to him. Flies were buzzing around him almost covering his face. All this we gleaned with just a brief glance for the sight and smell were so terrible that we only gave it a quick look and then moved on. It's difficult to identify a body in such a disfiguring state, even its nationality.

We casually hiked along the dusty, winding road in our usual carefree manner. The sun was high. The road was dry with tall grass growing on each side. Suddenly we came upon a squad of our own infantry headed in our direction. They were crouched on each side of the road with rifles poised for reaction to whatever this was that was headed in their direction. Their stern somewhat disgusted looks had a sobering effect on us, causing us to wonder if we should be going out into this area. But then we spotted a cave on the side of a cliff, halfway up a steep hill. Despite the many dangers, being the adventurous types, we decided to have a look. Part way up on this hot, difficult climb, we were able to get a panoramic view of the area. Below was a fairly open field and some bare ground mixed with occasional clumps of tall grass, with small hills in the background. Clusters of various types of trees and bamboo dotted the landscape. From this elevated spot we could see a hut below, which had been hidden from our view on the road by heavy growth of trees and brush. This, we decided, could be much more interesting than the cave and certainly much easier to reach.

It was a typical Philippine hut, bamboo supports with woven palm-branch covering, a window on each side, and one doorway. None of the houses had doors. It was bigger than most of the single-room huts we had seen in the area near our campsite. In the yard was a wooden bucket and bench. Two scrawny chickens scattered as we approached.

After all the stupid chances we had already taken, this time we decided on caution. As our approach to this dwelling was from the rear, we decided it would be best if one of us would go one way, another the other way, and the third man would swing way around and come in directly to the front, that being the only entrance.

Dymond headed off to the left, I went around the other way, and Gross took the long route around to where he could come straight in. At just about the same time, all three of us came into the clearing in front of the building and only our inexperience and the fact that none of us was what could be termed a "quick draw" prevented our shooting each other. I went into the building first and took the room to the left, while Dymond and Gross followed and explored the other rooms. "Hey, guys, look what's in here," I yelled. There, lying face-down, sprawled across the floor, was one Jap soldier. "Use your bayonet, stick him!" one of the guys said. "You know what they told us, make sure he's dead."

Landing on Leyte Island, Philippines—October 20, 1944

"You do it, not me!"

"Not me either!" He sure looked dead. We convinced ourselves that he was dead. Either way, we didn't care to stay to find out. We just did not have the stomach to plunge a knife into a human being, dead or alive. We left the place and continued on our exploration journey. There was no incentive to get back to camp since there was nothing for us to do there. It was, to put it plainly, one heck of a mixed-up mess with no one knowing what to do, supplies not arriving, and no food of any kind.

Off to one side of the road was a shallow pond, which had been created by the steady rain of the past few days. Here was a most peculiar sight—a horse with all four legs pointing skyward. The stench that came from that dead animal was by far the worst smell any of us had ever experienced. The odor not only choked and gagged us as we hurried along, but it seemed to follow us, permeating our clothing. When we rounded a bend in the road, we came upon a collection of stables. The roof, sides, and back were wooden walls with various partitions, but open on the roadside, with straw on the floor. There were some books, papers, and personal effects scattered about as well as harnesses and horseshoes, but no horses. It explained the presence of the dead animal. Obviously the Japanese unit assigned to defend this sector was a cavalry unit.

Our enemy had unintentionally supplied us with a lot of equipment, including some for our first recreational activity—horseshoe pitching.

When we got back to camp, we learned that we were soon to relocate to a site further north near a place called San Roque where we would set up our radar and continue operating. It would be a relief, away from all the clutter, commotion, filth, and the death smells at the landing site.

Chapter VI

Moving Forward

Just at dusk, a flight of enemy planes would come swooping in to attack our landing site. It was a regular, nightly occurrence from the first day of our landing in the Philippines. Searchlights would flash on, illuminating the sky, and the anti-aircraft guns would commence firing while the Jap planes dove in to drop their bombs and strafe the area with gun fire.

Our job was manning our radar set, reporting the approach of these enemy planes, giving constant updates, including location, distance, and direction. Now that they were here, we could do no more than just take cover wherever possible and watch.

Leaning against the sandbags that enclosed the men and their searchlight, I recalled my time of training for just what was happening. After basic training in North Carolina, I was assigned to the Army Air Corps. This was considered the most prestigious branch of the army. But when I learned that I was to be sent to ground observer school, I was not so sure of my good fortune. Each ground observer unit was comprised of three men who would be sent forward of the main line with binoculars, a hand-cranked generator, and a portable radio to locate and identify any aircraft, relaying their findings to headquarters. This ground observer training school was at a small Army Air Corps base located in the quiet little town of Orlando.

General George Kenney, MacArthur's airman, while the fighting was in progress in New Guinea, realized that early warning of air attacks was his first priority. What he needed were men on the ground to give him that early warning.

With flash cards and a projector screen showing silhouettes, we had to learn to identify the plane's type, make, and number as well as its country. It was not acceptable to say that it was a bomber. What kind of bomber—medium, pursuit, heavy, dive, torpedo, attack, patrol, or scout? Some planes were easy to identify—the PBY (Catalina), a seaplane, short and fat with a big boat for its bottom; and the P-38 (Lightning), with its dual fuselage. During that six-week course, some period was spent outside the classroom. Planes would fly over at different altitudes and it was our job to determine the plane's location, direction, and approximate elevation.

One week was spent in the field, sleeping in pup tents, practicing our scanning and radio operating. That radio was the only contact the three of us had with the rest of the company.

Returning to Drew Field, Tampa, Florida (our main base), after the ground observer training, I was assigned to radar school. During those air attacks in New Guinea, it was further determined that there was a more urgent need of radar operators than ground observers. To me, radar seemed preferable to camping out in enemy territory.

Leyte Gulf was full of ships unloading their cargo of men and equipment. The beach area was strewn with this material waiting to be moved forward, making us prime targets in a very vulnerable position.

No amount of learning is ever wasted. I had thought that by becoming a radar operator with my head inside a tent and my eyes glued to the screen, watching the blips, there would be no need for me to actually see the planes. However with my knowledge of planes, I was able to identify each one without even seeing the markings—the red circle or the star and stripes.

To us, the very word *Mitsubishi*, became synonymous with enemy aircraft. Every plane with that red circle was not just an enemy plane, but a Mitsubishi, the symbol of that cursed, dirty, Jap war.

As I watched the tracer bullets chasing each other up into the darkening sky, I marveled at the beauty of this show that seemed to rival any fireworks display, obliterating in one's mind all the pain of war.

While this air show was at its height with all its man-made lightning and thunder, I stayed close to the sandbags for the little protection they provided. Adding to this pandemonium and confusion were all the ear-shattering explosions. So much was happening all around us. Men were getting equipment, unloading and relocating it, and moving everything forward as quickly as possible.

The searchlight crew's job was to get a fix on a plane with its light so that the gunners could blast it out of the sky. The searchlight crew that I huddled next to could take credit for the demise of one Jap Zero without any assistance from an anti-aircraft team. They had locked their beam of light on one Jap fighter plane which was desperately trying to escape that brilliant illumination. The pilot of that plane kept maneuvering his craft lower and lower in his attempt to escape that light, which was so bright that we could actually see the pilot. That crew did a masterful job, keeping their light locked right on him, dropping the light as the Jap kept flying lower in his effort to get back into the darkness. Then came a big splash and a cheering from the searchlight crew as one Jap plane was gone. Darkness made it impossible to see what happened to the Jap, but there was no time to be wasted. The light crew quickly resumed the search for more planes.

During all the confusion, I noticed that one of our anti-aircraft guns was firing at a plane that I easily identified as a P-38 with its dual fuselage. No other plane in any other country had such a plane with two fuselages. I heard someone screaming at them that they were shooting at one of our own planes. They stopped firing and explained that they knew it was a P-38, but "That other anti-aircraft unit was firing at it."

The Japs left after having done their damage for that night, but they would return again the next night. With each passing day we were better established, more entrenched, disbursed, and well prepared for the next attack.

As days passed, we became more settled into somewhat of a routine. Tension lessened to where we could feel adjusted to a degree, with a better grasp of what to expect.

A few days later we had our first contact with the USMC. Our attention was drawn to a commotion just down the beach from our camp. With nothing to do in camp, a bunch of us moseyed down that way to see what was happening. A group of photographers was setting up their cameras on the beach in preparation for some filming. These men had come in from one of the many ships anchored in Leyte Gulf, had spread their gear out in the shade of the palm trees just where the sand met the beach grass, and were obviously planning to photograph something. A crowd was beginning to form, so it was obvious that we were not the only curious spectators.

Just a week before this day had been A-day, October 20, 1944: H-hour was 10:00 A.M., and our ship had beached later in the afternoon. The fighting was now up in the hills, so our area was pronounced secure. General MacArthur had come ashore with President Sergio Osmena. We had listened to their speeches on our small radio. Our time was now spent routinely operating our radar set or doing what we could to improve our living conditions. We were still sleeping in foxholes and getting little food. Our meals were D rations (a hard chocolate bar) at noon and K rations (cheese and crackers) at night, occasionally supplemented with C rations (the two-can fare of hash and hard tack).

"Action!" one of the men called out as the camera crew began cranking. Out in the gulf we could see small landing craft circling until all was ready. Then once lined up, on they came together, charging right up onto the beach. It seemed like a re-enactment of what we had experienced with the army the previous week.

The ramps on the landing craft dropped, splashing in the surf, and the men in full gear, packs on backs, rifles on the ready, came dashing forward, wading ankle deep through the water onto the sand. It was a Marine unit. Some of the men were throwing themselves flat as they reached shore, aiming their rifles toward the island's interior and also in the direction of the cameras. Others were running past the photographers and on into the trees beyond. More men from the landing craft kept coming and repeating this same scenario while the first group of men was standing around in the shade of the palms, behind the cameras.

That was it! The show was over. They folded the tripods and secured their gear, then prepared to head back on one of the many small boats. We looked at each other, shrugged, rose from our sandy theater seats, and headed back to our camp, all the while wondering what it was all about.

Could this have been for use as a training film? Maybe it was intended as recruitment material. It could have been a drill preparing for action on some other beachhead. A study of the film back at their base might be used to show each man what he had done right or wrong. But why here?

Of course, after what we had already been through in the real action with so much death and carnage, our cynical thoughts suggested to us tomorrow's newspaper headlines reading, "Marines Have Landed in Leyte; Beaches Are Now Secure."

Finally the time came for us to relocate our camp. In the early hours, we loaded our gear on our platoon's truck and headed north on the narrow, dusty road. This new location at San Roque was on a beach, just made for swimming, with a smooth gradual slope into the water. The waves were just slowly rolling in and out. It was refreshing during the sunny days, but even more so in the evening hours when the water wasn't quite so warm. In this location we

Filipinos helping us build a hut at San Rouque—
No longer living in pup tents

had the feeling that this could have been a Sunday afternoon picnic at the local beach back home but for one very different reason—this was war and there was that Jap body lying there. He was there on the beach when we were assigned to this new site.

Our camp was situated three miles north of the landing site, and we were at last settled into doing our job, continuously scanning by radar for aircraft activity. We could relax on this beach, which showed no signs of damage from the war. It was so unlike the overcrowded landing area where we had spent two weeks sleeping in foxholes and getting food when and where we could. At last we could remove our dirty clothing and wash in a stream. This new location could have been easy, even peaceful, and more relaxing as we worked to build our camp but for the body of that dead Jap.

The wounded were usually carried off as soon as they fell. The dead were removed by the burial detail, in most cases just as quickly. But occasionally one would be overlooked. Such was the case with this Jap body on the beach so near our campsite. Actually it was on a direct line between our hut and the ocean, which tended to be very disconcerting on our dash to the water for a swim.

The sight and smell of a dead human being left exposed in the tropical sun defies description. The putrid remains rotting, stinking, and covered with flies presents a very horrid picture and this one was always in view. Unlike some of the many other dead we'd seen, this one was very different in that his head looked more like a skull with the leathery skin drawn tightly over all his bones. He appeared emaciated. We assumed that he must have washed ashore either from a ship or plane and had spent some time in the water.

Army regulations would not allow us to bury any of the dead. Nor were we allowed to even move one. To our messages informing them of this human debris, the reply was merely, "We will get to it, as with so many others, as soon as we can." We spent many hours agonizing over what to do about this human litter until we realized that there was no directive stating that we couldn't cover it up. We piled sand over him as one would have done back home with a smelly old dead seagull. We created a big mound of sand and marked the location so the burial crew would eventually find and remove it. This was a time when we were getting many rainy nights and the rain quite often washed away some of the covering sand, exposing an arm or a leg. Also the dogs that roamed so freely would quite often dig at our sand pile during the night. We would put more sand on the pile and continue to harass the authorities to come and remove him.

War leaves in its wake not just spent cartridges, damaged vehicles, demolished buildings, and discarded equipment, but the worst of war's trash—the bodies of men who had once talked, walked, and lived.

One morning we noticed that something had been digging at the mound and one of the hands was missing. That Jap was my enemy, and he would have killed me if he'd had the chance, but still I would have wanted him properly buried complete with all his parts.

Eventually they did come and haul him off. With our beach cleared and the warm ocean water so near, we really had it made! No one needed to feel sorry for us. Back home we knew our families were concerned for our safety and many others would still be feeling sorry for us, knowing we were in the Pacific war zone.

From that first day of our landing, we had had some very horrendous times, but later things calmed down for us. In our new location we settled into a regular routine, scanning by radar for aircraft activity. Much of the fighting had moved to the other side of the island.

Our radar set and camp were situated in a palm grove on a most beautiful beach. It was a narrow strip of land with the Leyte Gulf on one side and behind us was a stream fifteen feet wide and one to three feet deep, slowly flowing parallel to the shore until eventually it emptied into the gulf much further up the beach.

During that period we actually felt a bit guilty about our soft life, knowing that others were still having a very rough time of it. Not that we didn't have to take cover now and then from air attacks and be constantly alert for enemy infiltration, but it was a very relaxed time with our only chore a regular shift on the radar set.

The swimming was great and we could avail ourselves of that pleasure at any time of the day or night when not on duty. Being a very hot climate, we wore very little clothing and could run into the water whenever we felt the urge.

Young, healthy, and full of ambition, sleeping on the ground under pup tents was not for us. We decided we needed better accommodations. Back at the original landing site where supplies were continuously being unloaded, we were able to acquire some good lumber from discarded packing cases. We used the lumber for flooring and framing of our new home. Our first attempt to copy the native houses, which were made of palm and bamboo, was a disaster. In the Philippines bamboo grows to three inches in diameter, so it makes for sturdy construction in the native homes. Palm branches are split and then the leaves are woven by twisting every other one backward. We just could not seem to get the knack of it until a native came along, offering to help. Grasping the branch at the outer end, with one quick flick of the finger he split the palm. He gathered the rest of his family and offered to help with the construction. The women would do the weaving, sitting on the ground holding the branch down with one bare foot while a cigarette dangled from the corner of their mouths. Each branch once woven became a shingle. The men nailed some of the palm shingles to the sides and wired others to the roof. Being associated with the signal corps we had plenty of wire. The five of us, (Gross, Dymond, Odell, Garretson, and I) gathered up a pile of clothing (those worthless undershirts had real value), which the natives gratefully accepted as generous compensation. When finished, our building measured ten feet by eighteen feet with one window and doorway, both opening in the front. The roof did leak at first, but a few more of those palm shingles fixed that.

With the lumber we had left, we built a table and benches, a washstand, and a rack for our mess kits. I even made a saltshaker out of bamboo. We'd had enough of sleeping on the ground, so I made a bed by using bamboo for frame and legs, with burlap from old sand bags fastened over the frame, weaving wire through the overlapping areas. Even my nights were restful.

Seated at our newly constructed picnic table, there were card games, usually pinochle, and letter writing while we munched on raisins and cheese, which we had swiped from a nearby mess tent.

The slow-moving creek out back was ideal for washing off after a swim in the salt water. It was also great for washing our clothes after living so long in the same dirty uniform. We preferred not to follow the natives' method of beating their clothing with rocks, finding that our strong soap worked better. One day while standing out in the middle of that three-foot deep stream washing my extra pair of pants, Dymond came down to the water's edge and began throwing coconuts to splash me. Returning them just as fast, I forgot about the pants that were soaking, which the stream carried away.

Gross was keen on physical fitness, having spent much time in the gym back in Detroit, so he and I put up a chinning bar, made a punching bag out of old sand bags stuffed with palm leaves, and even found an old basketball hoop and made a backboard for it. It gave us all the opportunity to work off our youthful energy.

The Japs had protected this beach area with interlocking World War I type trenches in the sand. Tired of jumping over them as we moved about our camp area, we got a lot of exercise filling them in wherever they intersected our paths. A lot of our time was spent with a shovel, digging slit trenches or garbage holes. Back home we might say "digging to China," but as we were on the other side of the globe, we were digging our way home. When Dymond, who came from Pennsylvania, found a piece of coal, he exclaimed that he was almost home.

Another lesson learned in New Guinea was the added distance our planes could travel by adding auxiliary tanks, thus surprising the unprepared Japs. These spare droppable wing tanks, when empty, were ejected from the planes into the ocean. Gross and I got two of these pontoon-shaped tanks when they floated ashore and made a boat for ourselves by slicing the larger one down the middle and fastening the two halves, one on each side of the smaller one. We then had our own floating P-38 complete with seats and paddles, so we could row across the stream to see the movies they were having in that big camp over on the other side.

Occasionally we would hitch a ride to Tacloban, the capital of the island, where some enterprising locals would have roadside stands selling native craft. Like most of the rest of the island, all of the buildings there were in very bad condition.

I spent some time with two Filipino boys, Domingo Loyoloyo (fifteen years old) and Francisco Canas (eleven) trying to create a Filipino/American dictionary. After a time, I dropped the project because of their accent and my spelling.

Pigs, dogs, chickens and other creatures roamed freely, since there were no fences or pens in the Philippines. Gross and I caught a chicken one day and tied it to a post. The poor thing was just bones and feathers, but we had hopes of fattening it up as a possible supplement to our diet or maybe even the chance of finding an egg some day. After a week of patiently waiting, we gave up and set it free. But after being fed so well it wouldn't go away. It followed us everywhere we went and it would even jump up on our laps.

Before we were re-assigned to a new area, an air corps unit was sent in as part of the army of occupation, locating their camp next to ours. They fussed constantly about being assigned to this area that, according to them, was still much too dangerous. They had no idea of what we had been through before this new life of tranquility. We secretly tapped into their generator, which gave us one more luxury—electric lights.

The army must have figured it was getting to be too civilized for us, and our life of leisure was over. It was time to move on. It had been a whole month of incredible peace and industry—a sharp contrast to any other time during the war. Life had not been easy for us before this period and would get worse later, but for a brief time we had it made!

Chapter VII

Ormoc

We waited in the dark seated on top of our equipment and supplies, which we'd loaded onto our platoon truck the previous night. Our driver could not start up until there was morning light enough for him to see the road. We were never allowed to have any light showing for fear of giving the enemy a target.

The day before, we'd received instructions to relocate on the west coast of Leyte near a place called Ormoc. Because those orders had come late in the day, we'd had to work into the night packing, taking down the radar set and storing it in its case, folding up the cook tent and headquarters tent, and picking up and loading all our gear on the truck. It was well after 1:00 A.M. as I hauled the heavy crates to the truck and I was getting very tired. When I looked around in the dark, I realized that not many of the crew was still working. My bunkmates had slipped away and were fast asleep in our hut. They had been sneaking off one by one without my noticing, but I'd been brought up to not quit a job until it was finished.

There wasn't much rest that night for any of us because we were roused early in the morning. We hated to leave our comfortable shack and all the other things we had built. Hauling our stuffed duffel bags and other personal items to the truck, we'd climbed up on top of the load to wait.

At five A.M., our convoy started moving, just as the sun was coming up. Our truck was positioned in the middle of the convoy, which was comprised of six trucks, with a jeep in the lead and another jeep in the rear. Each jeep was equipped with a heavy caliber machine gun. Guns were also mounted over the cab of each truck.

We headed south on the narrow coastal road. Usually whenever we traveled on the island's dirt roads we sent up a cloud of dust, but this day the road was wet from all the rains of the previous weeks. At Dulog our convoy halted. The road ahead had literally disappeared under a large expanse of water. Only by the dense growth of trees standing knee-deep in water could one calculate where the road must be. We waited on our very uncomfortable seats atop the loaded truck while the officers met in conference. Apparently, since there was little choice, the decision was to move forward slowly, following the leader, trusting that the wheels would meet some firm ground beneath all the muddy water.

All the vehicles used in the Southwest Pacific amphibious operations had been modified to fit the terrain. Among the modifications was a change to the exhaust pipes, which were angled vertically from the vehicle, enabling them to operate in fairly deep water. Occasionally as the trucks drove off the landing ships, they might drop into deep water.

At this juncture in the road, our greatest concern was mud, an ever-present danger that our truck could be stranded, mired in thick, gooey mud. Very slowly our truck moved out, following along with the rest of the convoy. It was a very tense ride for us; we felt every odd motion the truck made. Any moment we feared we might be thrown from the truck and have to swim.

After finding the road again beyond the lake of water, there were still several miles of skidding and sliding in the muddy ruts before the land eventually began rising as we approached Abuyog, where we were to pick up the road that led up into the mountains. This was the only route that actually crossed the mountain range, which ran north and south along the center of the island. The only other route to Ormoc would have been along the north coast of Leyte, but at that time that area was still being hotly contested.

It was 9:00 A.M. when we began our ascent into the mountains. It had taken four hours to go that first twenty miles along the east coast, partly because of the flooded roads, but in many cases, because an impassable bridge would force our convoy to wallow through the rocky streams to get to the opposite side. There were no rivers on the island of Leyte, but many streams carried water from the mountains to the shore. The retreating enemy had blown up many of the stone bridges that crossed those streams. Each truck had to drive down the bank, slowly maneuver across the stream, and then climb the opposite bank. Perched high on top of the truck as it swayed side to side, we hung on, holding our breath until we were safely on the road again. Although no vehicle tipped over, each time we maneuvered down the steep bank, crossed the rocky stream, and then struggled up the other steep side, we had many instances when we thought we were going over.

The sun was bright, so we knew it would be another hot day. As we climbed up into the mountains, the narrow winding road curved almost back onto its original course with elongated Ss as we went higher and higher. The driver had to frequently downshift the truck, which groaned on the steep climb, as it inched forward. It was hot in the mountains, but a steady breeze made the ride somewhat tolerable. Some of the guys lay on the baggage sleeping or just relaxing.

At noon, we stopped at a high peak while K rations were passed out, and we got a chance to get off of the truck and move about, although we were cautioned to stay close. The tall waving grass in the fields and the close growth of trees in the forested areas made ideal conditions for an ambush, but the view was spectacular. Rolling hills with green-tree covering spread out in every direction, unbroken by any manmade obstruction. It resembled an undertaker's fake grass, covering waves of rolling hills. Even with the quiet beauty, we had to be constantly on vigil since there was no way of knowing where the enemy might be.

In the hot damp climate of the Philippines things rust and mold very quickly. On a scavenging foray a week before this, I had found a priceless treasure, a one-gallon tub of heavy grease. It would provide protection not only for my rifle and knife, but would aid in keeping my boots dry. I guess I was careless, though, when I loaded my bucket of grease on the truck,

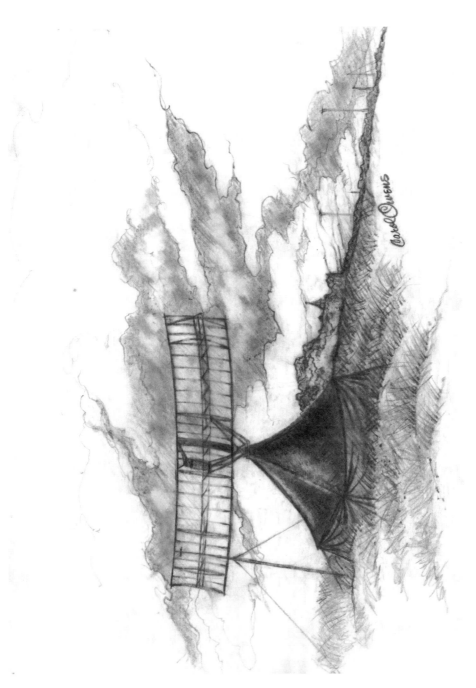

Our Radar Set

for as we bumped and jolted along, my friend Dymond's duffel bag fell onto my open bucket. It didn't penetrate much since the grease was so thick, but it did leave a greasy mess on the bottom of his bag. Sensing Dymond's irritation with me as he scraped the grease from his bag, I took my wonderful bucket of grease and flung it from the truck. It was my subconscious intent, I think, to demonstrate to him that his friendship far outweighed the value in that bucket. A little later he handed me one of his bananas. No spoken word was necessary. We were family.

At two in the afternoon, as we reached the outskirts of the coastal town of Baybay, our convoy was halted again. We had been impatiently looking forward to reaching the town where we had been promised a chance to get down from our miserably uncomfortable seats for a brief stretch and an opportunity to get some water.

While we wondered what was happening and why the halt, it took some time for word to travel along the line back to us. The lead trucks were under fire from some Jap snipers in the trees. We were told to just sit tight as more time passed while the Japs were unceremoniously dislodged from their treetops.

During the entire journey, this was the only contact we had with the enemy. We learned later that another convoy that made the trip on that same route just after we did was ambushed and very badly mauled, even though they had army tanks in front and rear for protection. We never found out why we got through so easily. We speculated that the enemy may have been waiting for a bigger target. I guess we just were not important.

In Baybay the natives came out to see us, waving and shouting greetings. The houses were fairly close together, simple wood frame structures painted white with picket fences and covered wells in the front yard. It seemed that no area of the island was just like any other. They cheerfully pumped water from their wells so we could fill our canteens, offering us the only thing they had, but it was not just water, it was wonderful COLD water! Ice water could not have tasted better.

On the route north from Baybay, in many areas we could avoid the bomb-pitted roads and demolished stone bridges by driving along the beaches. The trip from Baybay to Ormoc was approximately thirty miles, which we covered in just three hours, reaching Ormoc at 5:00 P.M.

Our first night in Ormoc was spent in the Seaside Hotel at the shore end of a pier that reached out into Ormoc Bay. Our stay at this hotel was not the vacation site that one would write home about. Although before the war this four-story building must have been a very impressive structure, at the time we got there, it was just a shell. It had lost its roof, the exterior walls were full of holes, there weren't any furnishings, and plaster and other debris littered the floors. We nailed together some sticks to make an improvised ladder which we used to climb up to the second floor. Using shovels, brooms, and scraps of wood, we cleared away a place where we could spread out our blankets. I usually had no problem sleeping, but that night the men on the first floor, part of the headquarters team, worked throughout the night. The wind was making a mournful sound through the many holes in the walls and plaster was still falling from the walls onto the floor above us. In addition to all that, I found the wooden floor to be much harder than the ground to which we had become accustomed. I grabbed my blanket, climbed down the ladder, and found a clearing on the ground in the motor pool. In spite of my concern that a truck might pull out in the night and I would not be seen by the driver, I slept until sunrise.

While we waited to learn of our next move, Gross and I got a chance to do some exploring of the area. We never were content to just hang around camp. Maybe it was my inquisitiveness, but Gross usually went along with it. We walked over to what had once been the town of Ormoc. It had been laid out with real streets in checkerboard pattern and buildings of brick. It was so unlike the native huts of palm and bamboo that were near our camp on the east coast of Leyte, scattered around in no special pattern. The entire area was just rubble from the navy shelling of the whole Ormoc grounds. We took a short cut across one block even though it was difficult walking with the ground so littered with debris. We casually strolled through, kicking aside some of the bricks and other trash. As we shuffled along talking, we noticed a military sign on the roadside at the far end of the block. The printed matter was facing the other way. When we finally reached that road where we could read the sign, we stopped, immobilized, and looked at each other, afraid to even lift one foot, for it read: *Keep out! This area is heavily mined!* We decided, henceforth, to stick to the roads. No more short cuts.

The day before Christmas we were instructed to establish our camp on the hill just on the outskirts of Ormoc near a boys' vocational school, which, like all the rest of the area, was just a shell. We set up our tents near these damaged buildings. It was hard to visualize what the whole area might have once looked like for it had been so severely damaged by the fighting and the bombardment before the Americans had landed. The terrain showed indications that it had been well landscaped, with flowerbeds and neatly trimmed shrubs, but not so now. With the bombing and so many dead, it was anything but a pleasant sight. There were so many bodies on that hill that the only recourse had been to use a bulldozer to push the bodies into one of the bomb craters. Arms, legs, and other body parts protruded from that sparsely covered hole, still visible if one looked in that direction. The stench was by far the worst. That bomb crater was an open hole, filled with pieces of human beings—human refuse. But it was not a still, unmoving, quiet grave. That hole, full of human remains, was like a wound on the face of the earth, with all that is associated with a horrible infection. But the odor that that wound emitted was overpowering, sending forth a smell that would cling to one's clothing and remain in the nostrils of the living. We had to sit huddled over our mess kits, keeping the flies away while we quickly consumed our skimpy meals. I was not a smoker, but I kept a lighted cigarette close to me in an attempt to overcome the smell with smoke and also hold back the hordes of flies.

There on that hill, exhausted from the arduous work of setting up our camp, I lounged on the ground, hot, sweaty, and dirty. I watched the antenna on our radar set, with its various protruding metal strips, turning slowly as it scanned for aircraft. The antenna was covered with flies, clinging to each metal branch. Flies so thick that there was no empty seat. I saw one fly slowly circling their parking lot as if watching for an empty space to light.

The sun was just going down as one by one we gathered outside our tent, tired, not eager to talk or even to listen, and too tired to sleep. We sat or reclined on the ground with still some light, the moon just coming up. We could make out the figures of each other, shadowy images in that dim light. It was all so quiet, with each man to his own thoughts. It was an eerie quiet after all the exploding noises of the previous two months. I sat up, wrapping my arms around my knees, feeling a lump in my throat. No word was said until someone in the still darkness spoke aloud what every guy was probably thinking: "Hey, this is Christmas Eve." More stillness, then in the dark a voice said, "Yeh!"

Chapter VIII

Swamp Camp

It is difficult to comprehend, even for those of us who lived it, how little information we were given concerning our movements during World War II. In peace-time, the military man is told not only where his next assignment will be, but even given some limited choice and time to prepare for the move.

We were in a perpetual state of quandary, with seldom an answer. We would eventually learn what was happening and where we were going—after the fact upon arrival at our destination, or in some cases, years later.

News reporters would be sending their reports to their home office, which we might learn about later in letters from home.

There never was a lack of speculation, gossip, or rumor. Mostly it was a guess, a rationalization fabricated from some scrap of whisper that someone overheard someone else say.

Yet despite this complete lack of information, we were never complacent. We always wanted desperately to know, but we seldom did.

With the proper training, even man can be programmed to function without question, to perform as directed. On Christmas Day 1944, shortly after we had erected our camp and set up our radar on that bloody hill in Ormoc, we were told to take it down. We were moving. Was a new site deemed better for reception? Had our officers complained about the sanitary conditions? Did this quick relocation have some other purpose? One thing we knew was that the move could not have been for health reasons, because our new location was even worse.

This site was right on the shore on the west coast of Leyte, just a couple of miles south of Ormoc. The beach was a very different beach from the miles and miles of soft sandy beach at our location on the East coast. This new site was on a rocky shore, with gradual slope, so strewn with various-sized rocks that it was difficult to walk down to the water's edge.

Our camp was set between the shore and an unapproachable swamp. The rank stink of decaying vegetation emitted an obnoxious odor from the stagnant, foul-smelling, shallow water. The area was crowded with a growth of bamboo, various kinds of scrubby brush, green scum, and close, stunted trees. It was inhabited by many kinds of flying and crawling creatures, creating a seemingly impregnable natural barrier. To us it was a barrier, but the enemy, the Jap, was not human. It would not have been a deterrent to him.

Also stranded on the shore was a disabled wooden Jap landing craft which seemed to stand as an ever-present reminder of war. Though long since abandoned, it created an eerie sense of Jap presence. It had been shot up when the enemy had brought reinforcements to this side of the island. All around the camp we strung barbed wire and installed sandbag-enclosed machine gun emplacements. It seemed more that we were being imprisoned rather than defensively protected.

A winding, treacherous trail led down to our campsite from the main road. Each time we maneuvered down that trail, we had had to twist and turn, avoiding ditches, trees, projecting land formations, and swamps while hoping that there would not be another vehicle coming in the opposite direction, making passing most difficult. If the driver were to slow or stop, we might not get going again. This was a stretch of about one mile, but what it held for me was far worse than curves and land irregularities. Once we had established our position, we set up our tents and our radar set and began scanning for enemy aircraft. This secluded area, though rather quiet during the day, held a dread for me on that ride through the woods to head-quarters and back to camp.

By this time we were hardened, conditioned, kill or be killed, don't care, seasoned GIs. "A dead Jap was a good Jap." We were considered army-trained killers. "If it doesn't stink, stick it." Many men had been shot or stabbed in the back because they had thought that the enemy was dead, not feinting death. Therefore, the instructions were, if in doubt, use the knife or bayonet to make very sure. It was the duty of the burial details to remove any dead. However, more importantly, they were required to examine the body for pertinent data that might give clues to enemy movements. We were prohibited from touching or even moving a body so we had always given the dead plenty of room with no intention of touching or moving any of them. Here was a very different situation, for across that trail to our camp was the body of one dead Jap. His body was lying across our tracks in an area where it was not possible for the truck wheels to avoid running over it.

From the first day that we had landed on the beaches of Leyte, we had seen so many dead. Dead in so many positions and so many states of decomposition, from dead that had just been shot to bones with only rag covering, the hot tropical sun causing the dead to turn blue and become bloated in only a few days. Flies in their eyes, their ears, filling the air, some bodies crawling with maggots before they could be buried. The stench was so terribly strong and the bodies in such a state that one could not tell to whose army they belonged. We were supposedly hardened, immune by this time to death's sights and smells, but twice each day we had to traverse that winding trail up to the main road and back. On each trip we had to drive over that body. The first few days, there was a slight bump as we met that spot in the road, but then as the days passed and the body flattened, we felt nothing. But I knew each time when we were nearing that spot, even when there no longer was any motion in the truck, for I could not help shaking as I gripped the seat and braced myself, prepared for the bump that I still felt. It was just another death, just one of so many. It had no life, yet it was still a human body. Can one become so insulated as not to feel?

When the burial detail finally did remove that body, I was not aware of it for I found that I had been closing my eyes and still bracing myself.

Japanese landing craft beached near our camp in Ormoc

The aura of death lingers on in all of one's senses and yet it is only a memory that exists within the mind that no amount of years can erase.

This camp area was so foul that whenever we got the chance to get away from it, we did. Even a trip to the dentist was preferable to staying there. However in one case it was actually necessary to leave, for I had a tooth that was giving me considerable discomfort.

After securing the necessary permission to leave, I set out walking along the beach on a circuitous route. Though it was a longer walk, it allowed me to avoid the road through the woods. It was about two miles to where the medical officers were located. It seemed to me that the dentist's tent was situated too close to the road where the constant truck movement was spewing their clouds of dust.

His tent was not very big, but adequate for his work and equipment, which took up much of the space. We were required to wait in line outside the tent. In some ways this reminded me of a barber shop (minus the reading material) where no appointment was necessary; just wait in line, move up, and then take a seat when the dentist finished with the previous patient.

Salt sprinkled on the ground was the only attempt made to keep down the dust inside the tent. One bare light bulb, located just over the patient's head, was all that illuminated the tent. The dentist had a metal tray with a cloth covering to hold his instruments. All his equipment was designed to be portable so that the whole operation could be moved with short notice. The drill was powered by foot, similar to the old sewing machine treadles. It didn't seem to be any less efficient, though, than the high-powered instruments of today.

He poked around in my mouth a bit, sighed, and said, "Can't waste a lot of time on that one, it's going to have to come out." It all went well until he asked me my outfit. I had said simply that I was a radar operator with a signal aircraft warning company. What happened next made me wish that he had put his instruments in my mouth before asking so I could not have responded because I was not prepared for the repercussions of my reply. A guy that was waiting his turn began yelling, "Why didn't we get any warning about last night's raid? What good is radar if they don't let us know that enemy planes are coming in?" That was just the beginning of his tirade, but by that time I couldn't have said more even if I had had an answer, for my mouth was full of dental instruments and my whole face was numb. His emotional outburst left me with a terrible feeling that somehow we had failed. Only later did I learn that the raid he was referring to had been carried out by two planes that had come in below radar detection. But knowing that we were unable to find and give warning of those planes did not remove my feeling of failure. A terrible sense of futility had me wondering if my being there made any difference.

We operated our radar set with the antenna scanning the sky while we watched the scope as it picked up a blip. We called our information into headquarters, giving them the exact grid coordinates. But did they already know of that flight of planes? Had another unit in another area already reported its location? Was it our own planes that they knew were there anyway? Did knowing of the approach of enemy planes make any difference? Did our information matter at all? Did I make any difference? It was not the tooth extraction that caused me pain that day. I tortured myself agonizing over that question—did I make any difference?

There are many stories of men who do some heroic deed, bucking the odds, showing their bravery, and are recognized for it with a medal acknowledging their act of courage. They know they had an effect. But very few are ever in a position to see the outcome of their act. We were constantly on the move, always close to the front lines with ever-present danger, sickness, shortages of food, catching sleep or rest when possible. Yet we could not see that what we did mattered. Did my being there affect anything?

Every day seemed hotter than the previous day. The oppressive humidity made even breathing difficult. The stench from the swamp made us ill while fitful sleep was possible only with mosquito-net covering, which was held above us with stakes nailed to each end of our cots. The shortages of food, the infestation of insects, the inability to wash, the scarcity of supplies, and the sweltering heat with overpowering humidity all lowered physical tolerance and morale, creating a challenge that could reduce anyone to the breaking point.

At this time, we had two twenty-man squad tents for the whole platoon, with standard army folding cots. The lieutenant had his own tent. The tent I slept in contained mostly radar operators. The other tent sheltered mechanics, radio operators, cooks, and medics.

We performed our various duties, some nights operating the radar, other nights assigned to guard duty, with one free night in four. We hardly spoke to each other for it took too much effort.

It occurred to me one day that I had not seen Pat Toranto, one of our mechanics, for some time.

"He went on the truck to headquarters back on the other side of the island."

It was several days ago that the truck had left. "When will be he back?"

"He's not coming back!" The way that the officer said it gave so much finality that clearly no additional information would be forthcoming and no more questions would be tolerated. That simple, straight-forward answer, "He's not coming back!" left little doubt as to what was wrong. If it were an accident causing an injury or a physical illness, it would have been explained at great length and it would have been easily understood, considering our condition.

It seemed to me that Toranto had been coping as well as any of us had. Maybe someone in that other tent noticed something. At this time there was very little interaction. We each tended to keep mostly to ourselves, subconsciously conserving what stamina had not been drained away. The oppressive heat had us functioning as zombies with very little individual communication. Also the monotony of duty in the close, stuffy radar tent, reading the blips on the scope and making our report of aircraft activity to headquarters, coupled with long hours of guard duty sapped what little energy we had.

Throughout those months that we were condemned to coping with that challenging environment, the only saving grace we had that gave us the strength to survive that ordeal, to maintain our sanity, and keep going was our youth!

Chapter IX

One Simple Act

The generally accepted rule of the road was to give a lift to anyone along the way who needed a ride.

This day we were in our company truck, getting supplies from headquarters so there was plenty of room in the back of the truck. I preferred riding back there where I could escape the fumes from our sputtering truck engine, avoid some of the road dirt, and at the same time get a better view of the countryside. The dust from so many vehicles constantly on the move was leaving a coating of tan on the palm and bamboo huts. All the houses, so similar, appeared as if they had stood for years, and yet they could be erected in the time from sunup to sunset.

The native Filipino people would gather to watch us as we passed by, in ragged clothing, bare feet, and little ones with no clothing at all. Their facial expressions spoke of sadness mixed with a sense of relief, eyes that could not even cry tears of joy, more a sense of weariness than jubilation and faces so full of questions. *Is it over? What next?*

We stopped to pick up a group of Filipinos, just one of many who were operating in guerrilla bands in the Philippines. The first words to me by one of the young guerillas, as he climbed up into the truck, had been "I ate a Jap liver." It was a boastful statement, said with obvious pride. It was easy to tell that he viewed his act as one of courage or complete domination over a tyrannical foe. To him, it represented an act of utter retaliation; the culmination of years of built-up hatred.

There was so much for which to be atoned. No longer was he the one who must grovel. The suffering had been the loss of loved ones, friends, and material goods. More pointedly, it was the anguish of humiliation, of the loss of dignity, honor, and self-respect. But this young man was also correct in assuming that his compatriots, even those in his own band, could not do what he had done. That was clear by the looks on their faces as he spoke those words, a mix of disapproval yet acceptance. It was a simple, straightforward remark, requiring no response. I was neither shocked nor racked with disbelief. My only unspoken fleeting thought had been, *Was it raw or cooked?*

It was not all that strange or weird in that other world. The constant sounds of gunfire,

far and near, and the peculiar stench of death that had begun for us on that day we had landed had intensified with time. No day passed without the presence of war attacking one or
more of our senses. The bizarre had become an ordinary, everyday way of life.

To some, death to the enemy was final, but to others it required complete triumph. The
killing act was not the end. This act of his was the fulfillment of a need, not just a desire for
satisfaction. It was an act done not for want of sustenance for the body, but gratification for
the spirit.

I did not analyze his act on that day nor form any judgment or question. I had not
thought of it as an act of cannibalism, yet in fact it *was* that. All he had said were just those
five words. Yet after all these years, I can still see him and hear the pronouncement his whole
being made. His jet-black hair, crowning his light tan skin, was waving as the truck drove on.
His clothing had become part of him—dirty, ragged shirt; loose, baggy pants; well-worn, scuffed
boots; and grenades at the waist, placed more for effect than use, along with the rifle that
was his manhood. All saying so clearly, "It's my turn now!"

Reflecting with time's retrospect and from a position of comfort, I wonder as much about
my own reaction that day as I do about his statement. At the time that he had climbed up
into the truck, I had been deep in my own personal thoughts. *Will I get a chance to wash today?
What hours will I have to stand guard duty tonight? I have to clean my rifle. What does lettuce taste
like? Does milk always come powdered?* Home and sanity were literally and figuratively on the
other side of the globe. The world I had known was clean, pure, and pleasant. World events
I had thought would never involve me, yet there I was in a new life in a different world. For
this young man, before the Japanese invasion and the battle for liberation, his world must also
have been serene or even idyllic.

When I hear someone say they know exactly how they would react in a particular situation under given circumstances, I think to myself, *Until you are there living, feeling, actually
immersed in that existence, you can only assume that you know.*

To forgive and forget was not an option for that young Filipino guerilla for the wounds
were too deep. Was it really an act of cannibalism or of supreme revenge? I could not judge
him then, nor can I now.

Chapter X

Four Dead and One Wounded

"He just stood there right in the middle of the road firing shot after shot at those flee-ing Jap soldiers." Gross, my buddy, was telling everyone in camp about our escapade and speaking of me as, "The bravest guy I have ever known." Well, I'm not one to argue with anyone, especially when they are saying such nice things about me, but it wasn't exactly like that. It was what would probably be considered stupidity, not bravery.

There was no reason to stay in camp and write letters home as no mail was coming or going. So since we had a chance to leave camp to scout around and see what was happening, we did. Our camp area was so poorly located next to that foul-smelling swamp that anywhere else would be a relief. Supplies were low, with food available for only two skimpy meals per day. We had finished our four-hour shift in the radar tent, which had begun at four in the morning. There was very little to eat that morning. I've never thought of hot dogs and sauer-kraut as breakfast food. Guard duty for us was not scheduled until evening, so off we went to get away from camp and see how our war was progressing. All over the world people would be reading their morning paper or turning on the radio to learn what was happening in the war in the Philippines. Our platoon was right on the front where it was all happening and we knew nothing.

I took my carbine as I always did. Gross got his rifle (an M-1) and helmet. When I kid-ded him about the helmet, because we never wore them around camp, he simply said, "If we go where I think you'll want to go, I'll need all the protection I can get." I laughed at that, but as it turned out, he surely was right.

Initially it was not our intent to go searching for the enemy even though we knew we were going beyond what could be construed as our own lines. We just wanted to see some-thing of what was happening in the area other than our own campsite. The sun was getting higher in the sky as we hiked along. It felt as if this was going to be another hot, humid day. Humid though the air was, the whole area, especially the road, was dry. As we ambled up into the hills, we agreed that we were probably the two biggest fools ever.

Along the roadside the growth was sparse. Here and there stood a tall coconut tree. Other areas had a thick growth of bamboo being crowded by palmetto plants and other greens that were unknown to us. After walking about a mile, we came to the small town of Cogol de Patag where we met a Filipino who told us that he worked for the US Army Intelligence. His assignment, he said, was to collect whatever he could find that would give clues to enemy activity. I was later admonished not to write his name on anything or discuss it with anyone, so I have long since forgotten his name. I think it was Jose, as it was a common name in the Philippines. We told him that we just wanted to see some of the countryside while we had some free time. He invited us to tag along with him, but first he had some friends he wanted to visit.

As we emerged from thick undergrowth into a clearing, we were completely unprepared for what greeted us. There stood the most beautiful, two-story Victorian house, with fancy carvings and multi-colored paint. Large decks completely encircled the big dwelling on both levels. The whole picture seemed out of place in this part of the country with all its palm and bamboo huts. It was like stepping back in time—a real Shangri La. The people standing on the porch as we approached the building were obviously of Spanish descent. It seemed as though they were left over or forgotten from the days when the islands were under Spanish rule. Their skin was whiter than that of the natives or even lighter than our tanned skin. The tall gentleman, obviously the patriarch, spoke briefly to Jose in Spanish, then turned to us and bowed slightly, a bit more than just a nod. He addressed us in perfect English, inviting us to come sit on their veranda.

Although the building appeared undamaged, one could tell that the family had had some hard times. Their dress, so different from the natives, though still regal, showed signs of wear. Small stains and patches with some mending gave clues to their attempt to maintain their aristocratic bearing. The two women, mother and daughter, dressed in ankle-length dresses, smiled pleasantly but never spoke. Either they deferred to the master of the house or maybe they were not versed in English. Once we were seated, a Filipino servant, not dressed as any native we had seen but with a smart white jacket and black pants, brought a tray with cut-glass goblets containing cold spring water, no doubt valuable belongings had been kept in hiding. Water was all that they had to serve us, but it was done with such a flair of dignity that it could have been their most-treasured last bottle of champagne. Gross glanced toward me, and without a word between us, I read his unspoken thoughts: *Don't drink the water!* We had been told that many times, but we raised our glasses together. We had no desire to offend those valiant people by rejecting their humble, though gracious, hospitality.

We had a pleasant visit, discussing many things. Our host knew no more of the progress of the war than we did, but from the actions and attitude of the Japanese he had seen in the area, it was obvious the war was not going well for our enemy. He spoke of being anxious for peace and a return to the life they had known. Times were changing rapidly for all of us. I had to admire this man, who stood so straight, with noble posture. He was the type you would like to get to know. I had the feeling that there was much I could learn from him. It was as if we had been in the presence of royalty. As we departed, the kindly old gentleman warned us that Japs had been seen in the next village, cautioning us because those still in the area were desperate men.

Leaving this congenial atmosphere, Gross, Jose, and I hiked along the road, another mile, to the next village, Tambuco. Jose learned from one of the town's inhabitants that 300 Japs had passed through their village the previous night. Those were not good odds for the three of us. As neither Gross nor I spoke or understood the language, we had no choice but to trust Jose completely, trusting in whatever he told us. His inquiries of the people in this village revealed that a group of guerrillas was planning on going up into the hills. Jose hurried us along to join them. We hesitated, but only for an instant. As we hiked along a dirt road, with eight guerrillas in front and four behind, or so we thought, Gross leaned over to me and said, "Don't look now, but we're being followed." When I turned around, I saw what appeared to be the entire male population of the town, totaling, I guessed, around 100, following. I wondered, was it curiosity to see what we were going to do, or did they feel a sense of security because now American soldiers had arrived, even if it was only two very dumb ones?

The crowd thinned out as we went farther from their village. Only fifteen of them had any form of weapon—some old Japanese rifles, a few knives, and anything else they'd picked up along the way.

The road up the hill wasn't particularly steep, but it was a steady climb and the sun was high, causing us to sweat. The surface of the roadway was dry with sparse growth of various tall trees and dull green growth crowding the edges. The Filipinos chatted among themselves as we hiked along. When everyone stopped, Jose translated for us. They had said simply, "Time for a break."

It amazed me how agile these people were. They would actually run up a coconut tree more easily than I could if it were lying flat on the ground. They must start learning to climb young; the little ones can probably climb a tree before they can walk. Our companions threw down many coconuts and with one deft swing of their knives, cut the tops off the fruit. Passing the open coconut around, each in turn drank some of the milk and then scooped out some of the soft mush with their fingers. Seeing the state of their fingers dipping out the coconut, I didn't feel all that hungry.

At this point, Gross and I began to have some real reservations about where we were. We figured it wasn't too late to turn back but as we would say later, we wouldn't have forgiven ourselves if we had not gone on.

Jose, with head held high, stepped out smartly, strutting confidently, feeling very important as he led the pack. He seemed almost cocky. He may have been showing off for us, or he may have felt a sense of importance being with American soldiers with whom only he could communicate. On our part, we were really beginning to wonder what we were letting ourselves in for.

Suddenly there was a sense of hushed tension within the group. They were all whispering nervously to each other. They moved around quietly, continuing to look in all directions, completely silent. Jose turned abruptly to us and explained quietly what all the uneasy excitement was about. "That hut off to the left of the road just beyond the tall grass with smoke rising above it would not be occupied by Filipinos; it has to be Japs." Later Jose explained that the family who had been living in that hut abandoned it, moving closer to the village where they would not be so isolated and exposed to Jap harassment.

"You're too tall," he said. "You go up the road behind that clump of trees by the road, out of sight of the hut, while we approach through the cogon grass." Then he scooted off to join the others before we could say anything. There was no time for discussion. We just did what he said.

We watched their movement with only the tops of their hats showing as they slowly advanced on the hut. Firing suddenly erupted and with it much yelling and thrashing with a great deal of commotion. The Japs, completely surprised, were fleeing as the guerrillas closed in.

Without warning eight Japs appeared on a dead run ahead of Gross and me up the road beyond the thicket. They crossed the road and raced across an open field. That was when I got the chance to fire. I guess when your life depends on it, you can really put on the speed, and those Japs were moving fast. I saw them for such a short time that it was not possible to aim; I could only keep shooting in their direction. I was able to get off eight shots before they made it over the rise. One of my shots hit a Jap in the knee. He dropped for a second and was then up and limping off, assisted by a fellow soldier.

With a carbine, you only need to pull back the bolt once and that will insert the first shell in the chamber. Then you can just keep pulling the trigger for rapid fire. With such sudden, unexpected agitation, coupled with my first sighting of the enemy, I nervously kept pulling the bolt back after each shot. I was, in effect, ejecting every other shell. When the excitement died down, one of the guerillas pointed to my unused shells on the ground.

In the meantime the guerrillas had reached the hut and were not interested in following the fleeing soldiers, for as Jose explained later, there could have been a whole company of Japs just over that rise. Four Jap bodies lay on the ground just outside the shack. The hut was a very low dwelling, the opening only about four feet, with the roof and sides thatched with the cogon grass. Jose showed us the freshly killed caribou that the Japs were cooking along with some sweet potatoes. The guerrillas salvaged what they wanted, netting them three more rifles. I picked up a helmet but wanted nothing else. Jose took what information he found on the bodies for army intelligence. He tore off their insignias of rank and their outfit patch from their jackets. Also he took name patches that were sewn to their shirts. Going through their pockets, he took what papers he could find.

As the natives had little in the way of clothing, they stripped the bodies completely naked. One member of the guerilla band found a pair of smart-looking leather boots on one of the bodies. Apparently in addition to his fatal shot, this Jap had also been hit in the foot and had bled into that boot. When the Filipino put his foot into his new boot, I could hear the slush of blood. But his satisfied grin was only an indication that his nice new boots fit. That was enough for us. It was time to head back to camp.

A few days later a directive came down via the chain of command from some important army people to our officer, Lieutenant McGowan, and from him to the two of us. It read in part, "Thank you for your enthusiasm, but in the future, stay out of our zone of combat, or your beneficiaries will be collecting your insurance."

Chapter XI

Jaundice

"We really need to do something about him. He hasn't eaten for several days. Just lies there." It took a long time for me to penetrate the haze, to shake the drowsiness, and come to the realization that I was the one they were talking about.

It was late January 1944 and we were still camped on the outskirts of the town of Ormoc near that terrible swamp. Though the actual fighting front was now a few miles north of our position, there were still the reports of infiltration by the enemy.

Every man had his turn at some hours of guard duty, day and night, posted in a sand-bagged enclosure with a machine gun. The nights were the worst, with the moon on the water telling a much different story from that which faced us in the dark, in the swamp in front. Except for those manning the radar set, the rest of the camp was in the tents, trying to sleep, but sleep did not come easily.

The man on guard was alone and felt completely alone, in the silent darkness. However, if he strained to listen, it was very clear, at least to him, that he was not alone. A little movement over there, some sound over the other way—a scraping, crawling sound, getting louder and louder. Now the noise was all around. Slowly he moved his hand to the gun, removed the safety, and lowered his body behind the sandbag shelter, just able to peer over the edge. But in that inky black darkness nothing could be seen. Still there was the movement. The crawling sound kept getting louder. The thoughts that filled his mind seemed to make it so very clear that the enemy was creeping up. They were approaching from the swamp. With this intense sound, it had to be a large force. They must now have penetrated the wire barrier. Gotta stop them! They're all around. They're coming in! Squeeze the trigger and let go a spray of bullets. "Take that, you yellow bastards!"

It was only sand crabs that move around at night. Yet each night was the same. Though you suspected it was those sand crabs again, with tense nerves and dark, humid nights, that noise would sound like the approaching of the enemy. We stood some hours of guard duty almost every night, but even on that one night in four that we were not on duty, our rest was shattered by the sudden blast from the guard's hand on the gun. He just couldn't take any chances.

In the daylight hours there were many chores to perform which we did as men in a trance. We didn't talk to each other. There was nothing to talk about and, besides, it took too much effort. Lack of nourishment and lack of rest, coupled with frazzled nerves, left us incapable of normal human responses. As food supplies dwindled, our meals were reduced. Meals twice daily were more than we cared for. With no replenishment of our needs forthcoming, only four items of food remained for the cooks to make into a meal—canned asparagus, dehydrated potatoes, sauerkraut, and hot dogs. The cooks did their best while working with this short stock of food. It was a balance that would sustain us, but with the heat, the damp climate, the tension, and the lack of sleep, there was little desire for food.

Christmas mail with packages had arrived in late January. That brown mush in the bottom of the mailbag, according to the letter, was a chocolate cake, although much of the writing on the letter had been washed away. It had been seven weeks since we'd had any contact with the outside world. A magazine that came in the mail was actually painful to look at with its pictures of people in fine clothing, maybe on their way to church. What would it be like to ride along a smooth road in that shiny car with its cushioned seats? Some days we'd just sit around and someone would talk about what he'd like to wear or what we would do when we got home.

They helped me up onto the truck, a Jap truck. Our platoon officer, Lieutenant. McGowan, loved to tinker with engines and had resurrected this abandoned scrap of iron with parts from other wrecks. He was very proud, and rightfully so, of having managed to get it running. It did give our outfit a second set of wheels, even though it was noisy, smelly, sputtered a lot, was somewhat unpredictable, and certainly very uncomfortable. It didn't have much to it but a seat for the driver and one passenger. I sat on a box on the flat bed in the back. There wasn't much for me to hold on to, but back there I wasn't subjected to the engine fumes, which in my queasy condition would have made the trip even more unbearable.

At headquarters we lined up for sick call. McNicholas, our sergeant, was in front of me in line. Thankfully the line moved quickly. The doctor, standing very erect and calm, was methodically snapping off his decisions after a question or two. Beside him was a small table where his assistant sat with paper and pen. Their set-up was in the open air, next to that badly damaged old hotel that was being used for shelter for the medical staff. I wasn't listening to what the doctor was saying. I had such stomach pains and weakness that all I wanted to do was to lie down. But they had brought me here and I sure needed some kind of help. It was Mac's turn next. "It's a touch of the flu and you're just about over it. Next." I only recall his looking intently into my eyes and I heard him tell the medic, "I'll take this one." I must have seemed incoherent, for he spoke instead to my buddies. "Get his personal belongings and deliver him to the 69th Field Hospital in Valencia." On the ride back to camp to get my things, we passed my buddy, Gross. To his questions, I told him the doctor had said, "Yellow jaundice."

Gross jumped back. "Is it contagious?"

"I just have it, that's all I know."

Jaundice results from a build up in the blood of bilirubin, a yellowish-brown substance that is normally extracted from the blood stream by the liver and excreted in bile. The liver performs a crucial and complex role in regulating the composition of the blood. So it's when the liver is unable to remove this bilirubin from blood rapidly enough that Jaundice results. Jaundice is most frequently brought on by anemia, causing a general loss of appetite, weight loss, nausea, vomiting, weakness, indigestion, and abdominal cramps. It may also cause inability to concentrate, impaired memory, confusion, and drowsiness, leading to coma as the condition worsens. To properly diagnose it would take blood studies, possibly a bone marrow study, A liver function test, A liver biopsy, and/or ultrasound graphics.

However, in the rubble that was Ormoc, there was no such medical equipment. Jaundice manifests itself in a yellow discoloration of the skin and pupils of the eyes. As we were taking daily doses of adabrine (an artificial substitute for quinine) to prevent malaria, our skin already had a light yellow tint caused by that preventive medication. The doctor could only make his diagnosis by the color of my eyes. The later stages of jaundice are cirrhosis of the liver or heart failure.

The forward hospital in Valencia was like all the other hospital areas on the island, a collection of various-sized tents with dust flying from the trampled ground. It was located close to the front lines for emergency treatment and preliminary care.

"That will be your bunk over there," the orderly said. From this point on there are many gaps in my memory as I was losing consciousness and getting weaker. When I awoke, it was daylight. It was that bell that had awakened me, a call to chow. It had been days since I had eaten anything and I knew if I was to survive, I had to force myself to get some food. Standing in the chow line, though, proved prohibitive in my unsteady condition. My legs could no longer support me. I staggered back to the tent where I collapsed on my cot. Another period of unconsciousness. My stomach was hurting and I was experiencing a complete loss of reality. This hospital area seemed full of activity but more like a dream. So much commotion and yet I neither saw nor talked with anyone and if anyone spoke to me, I was not aware of it. The whole scene was a fuzzy nightmare. A great deal of movement but with no realism!

"This hospital is being evacuated," the loud speaker sounded. I could not comprehend the meaning until the orderly said, "Get your stuff and get on that truck." They considered me a "walking patient," as I had no bandages, no signs of injury, and I had two legs. Somehow, I managed to get down to where the truck was waiting. I remember feeling a sense of relief that it was a small truck and I didn't have to climb up. The next thing I knew, I was on a ship, on a bunk in a compartment below deck. I don't know how I got there. Someone was exclaiming about the view as we traveled the long passage around to the other side of the island. I would have liked to have witnessed that scene, moonlight on the water with shadowy silhouettes of the island, the waving palms, and the ascending spray from the waves as they crashed on the shore, but my periods of consciousness were getting shorter. I was now beyond the point of being able to help myself.

At dusk, when I came to, I was in another hospital in Dulog and was receiving intravenous feeding. This was a very crowded medical tent. All the cots were set close together. A nurse was there moving around between the cots. I wished I could talk to her, the first American woman I had seen for so long, but she had no time. My cot was right on the edge of the wooden platform and I was getting some fresh air from the raised tent flaps. It was very hot and stuffy under that canvas. Later in the night, I felt drops of rain on my face. It felt so good, so cool, so refreshing, but someone was coming around dropping the tent flaps and I drifted off again.

The next day, they delivered me fifteen miles inland to the General Hospital at Burauen. The rain had turned dust to thick, gooey mud. This hospital area had been battling with this mud problem for some time, so boardwalks had been built all around from tent to tent, with wooden flooring in all the tents keeping us above the mud. To me, this area was a blessed oasis from all the nerve-shattering existence of the previous months, so quiet and peaceful with no dead bodies and no destruction in view.

The feeding I received through the veins must have instilled some life, for I was beginning to feel that I was returning.

In just two days I was able to stand and I wanted most of all to go to the shower and wash, to feel clean. There had been so few opportunities to wash in the preceding months. When I stood naked under the shower, I was shocked as I looked down at my body. I didn't realize how far down I had gone. My legs were only sticks with large bulges that had once been knees. My arms were bones with skin tightly covering them. My ribs were what shocked me the most, for they seemed to be actually protruding from my chest, so tightly was the skin drawn. My flesh, especially those areas not tanned, was a brilliant yellow in color. But in spite of my appearance, I felt good. I felt rested. I could stand. My mind was clear. I was even looking forward to my first meal at the mess hall. I was back among the living!

During the four weeks that they kept me at the hospital, I was able to see and feel much improvement. The quiet rest and good food, coupled with my youth, enabled me to begin covering my bones with flesh again.

The days were fairly uneventful—reading, writing letters, or playing cards, the usual army time-killers, were routine.

My stomach was in such constant pain, though, that it made it mandatory that when lying down, I would always have to lie on my side in a fetal position. The doctor's daily brief visits were, "How're you feeling?" check the chart, then on to the next bed. I saw the nurses more often. They would bring me a handful of pills, which included some painkillers, various vitamins, yeast tablets, and the most important cure for jaundice, good food. I was given specific instructions as to which pills to swallow at what time. Also, a large pitcher of water (with a glass) was placed on the stand by the bed with orders to consume the full amount before the end of the day. That pitcher of water stood as an ever-present demanding challenge.

Eventually the room service ended and trips to the mess hall became a new and exciting adventure. The PX was open for a just a few hours each day, but with very little money, it was just a window shopping excursion. The only thing I ever bought was a can of salted peanuts. Although my strict diet excluded them, I rationalized, convincing myself that the salted nuts would make me thirsty and I could, therefore, more easily consume that haunting pitcher of water.

News of what was happening in our war was scarce. We did learn that our forces had landed on Luzon. Another day we heard of the paratroopers descending on a POW camp and rescuing those prisoners. A few days later some former prison inmates were brought to our hospital. We saw them only from a distance because they preferred staying very much to themselves at the far end of the hospital compound. Men, women, and children of all ages seemed to shun association with the rest of the camp's inhabitants. Some of the men would get in the chow line, fill their tray, then get back in line, eating their meal as the line moved up, prepared to fill it again. Despite their extended stomachs and the doctor's warnings, those malnourished ex-prisoners couldn't seem to get enough to eat.

No matter how bad we may feel, there's always someone worse off. One day as I was feeling better, I was asked, along with several other guys, to help hold a man on a stretcher while they carried him from one place to another. He was obviously out of his head, thrashing around, making it difficult to contain him. As we deposited him with the doctors, I overheard one of the stretcher bearers aside, "He'll not live much longer." When I asked him, "What's he got?" he had said simply, "Jaundice."

So anxious was I to get back to my army family that when the doctor made his morning visit, I lied to him about my condition, flashing a bright smile and declaring, "I feel just great!" However, I did suffer many relapses after leaving the hospital and even when the war was over and I was home. But no one knew about my condition and as time passed, those spells became shorter in duration and farther apart.

The dictionary says of jaundice, "a disease." But a second definition speaks of distaste, hostility, and revulsion, just another definition of war!

Chapter XII

Volunteer

There was a time during my army life when I really knew fear. It was during that time in the hospital in the Philippines while I was recovering from jaundice. I was feeling better and regaining my strength, yet still quite weak.

While I was in the hospital, our platoon had moved from the west coast back to the east coast in an area not far from where we camped when we first arrived on Leyte back in October. I had a visit from Hartzheim, Sprinkle, and Hood, bringing me news of camp. They were now able to see some movies. It was just a projector lighting a screen out in the open, seated on the ground, but it was a big change. They'd been getting better food, too. In the verbal discourse and simple chatter, one fellow mentioned a rumor they'd heard that our outfit might be leaving the island of Leyte. This news, so casually spoken, stunned me. The thought that they might leave before I was released from the hospital had me wondering what I would do. I was beset with the fear of how would I be able to cope if they were to leave me here with strangers. How could I catch up with them if they were to leave the island of Leyte? Here was the clear reality of what existed but had not been spoken or even thought, how much we had come to rely on each other. We were a family. This was the real life. My other life on the other side of the globe was just a fading memory, so far away it was almost forgotten.

That casual remark that they might be gone when the time came for my release spurred me to act. Although I was still feeling weak, this period in the hospital with good food and comfortable rest was over for me. I could not take a chance of being left behind. It was not difficult to convince the doctors that I was fit and recovered enough to leave, as most of their patients wanted to stay as long as they could.

When I reached camp, I was re-entered into rotation, scheduled to assume my duties along with all the rest. Yet I was still struggling with the illness. On one particular night I had a recurrence of the jaundice while on guard duty. It hits the stomach and only by doubling over and bringing the knees up does the pain subside. So, while I was supposedly manning my guard post, in actuality, I was rolling around on the ground in agony. But no one knew.

If I thought this was going to be a restful time as we were no longer operating the radar,

I was in for a big surprise. In addition to guard duty, we were sent on many details. One day it was a trip to Palo to get gas. Another time to the Black Beach area to load rations on an LSM, or transporting boxes full of all kinds of equipment. One time it was our job to pile crates on a cargo net. We made a trip to Tanauan to pick up mail. We did stenciling of boxes and duffel bags at Rizal dump. One day I was assigned to be a runner. We had lectures on orientation. Some days I had to give a report to the platoon on what I knew about the progress of the war. They found plenty for us to do.

Occasionally we could catch the Singapore radio (Japanese held) station broadcasts, which had a very different version of the progress of our war. When our troops had landed on Leyte, they said it was "like throwing an egg against a rock." They reported that, "Because of economical and political disturbances at home, Roosevelt was forced to invade the Philippines." When American forces landed on Mindoro (after the island of Leyte was considered secure) they said it was because we were forced off the island of Leyte. When we landed on Luzon, the radio reporter said, "We are drawing the enemy into us, so it will be easier to annihilate them." Then in speaking of the Mindanao invasion, "The enemy has been thrown into confusion."

A call to stand formation in a war zone was unheard of, unlike life at a military post in the States where it was routine at the end of each day during the ceremony of lowering the flag. After all we had endured in the previous months, we felt this was our well-deserved rest period. So it was a big surprise to learn that we were to fall out at 16:00 hours in formation. The rest time had given me a chance to wash my other set of clothing. They were now clean and dry, so for a boost to my morale, when reporting for the formation, I put on my nice clean uniform, shaved, and brushed the dirt from my boots, and it did make me feel good about myself. Another unexpected ritual—the officer was actually going down the line inspecting the troops. Then an even bigger surprise for me came when he stopped in front of me and said to his assistant, "This one!"

Unbeknownst to me, I had been picked to stand guard that evening. "Why me?" In that hot tropical climate, I wasn't about to get my clean uniform all sweaty and dirty again, and no one was going to see me or even know where I was in the late night hours, so I put my other set of clothing back on for my scheduled tour of duty. But before we took our posts, the commanding general appeared with the officer who had picked me out, prepared to review the guards. When he got to me, he said to the accompanying officer, "This you picked as the best of the lot?" Nothing had been said that I had been chosen for this special duty because of my appearance nor had there been any mention that this was a special occasion with a visit by the general. I was not the only one embarrassed that day.

Though our area was considered secure, it was still essential that guards were posted and alert at all times. Not only because of the possibility of enemy infiltration, but because there was always the chance that some natives might be working as agents for the enemy.

Standing guard from midnight to dawn was the most difficult time. Any movement, any sound, would set one's senses on alert. It could be a small nocturnal animal on the prowl, but then it could also be the enemy. On some occasions, I was made corporal of the guard, so all I had to do was to post each guard, periodically check on them, and at the appointed time, change the guard. Then there were times when I was sergeant of the guard. That was the best, for all I had to do was stay at the command tent with nothing to do, unless a problem

| Schweibert | Lemont | Hartzeihm |
| Bensick | Dymond | Gross |

occurred. Fortunately, there never was one on my watch.

Early morning hours of guard duty in the Philippines watching the sunrise after a long, tiring, dark night were magical. Near dawn, the night would suddenly get darker. Then gradually it would lighten and silhouettes would appear. Shapes would begin to form as the sky brightened until finally the sun would slice like a knife separating earth from sky. It was morning again, the beginning of another day. Each time it happened, it was thrilling as the sun rose and darkness evaporated and with it the strain and tension slipped away. Camp would begin to stir as the world gradually awakened. I could see the cooks and KPs headed for the mess tent. Coffee would be ready by the time my shift ended when my relief arrived. All I craved was that hot cup of coffee before heading for bed. Fortunately, caffeine has never disturbed my rest and after a long, stressful night, sleep came easily.

Once in the mess tent, I would stick my canteen cup under the spout, get my coffee, and take a seat on one of the rough benches. It had become routine for me each morning right after guard duty. Drinking coffee black, though, was not to my taste. I had to have the cream and sugar.

One day when I reached the mess tent for my habitual coffee, there was no more cream. However, there was milk for the cereal and that worked almost as well.

The following day, they ran out of milk. But there was a powered product they called milk. If the coffee was hot enough and you did a lot of stirring, it worked pretty well, although you usually found some lumps at the bottom of the cup.

When the dry milk ran out, I resigned myself to drinking it black, as long as it was sweet. On the day supplies dwindled to where there wasn't any sugar, I sat for a while holding my very black coffee until I spotted a jar of strawberry jam. With big scoops of jam mixed well, it sweetened the black liquid. Not quite as good as sugar, but it was better than nothing. But the day the supply department substituted orange marmalade for the strawberry jam, I quit drinking coffee. Marmalade is not a sweetener.

That old army expression, "Hurry up and wait" was so true for us at this time. It was a waiting period, somewhat relaxed, but definitely not restful.

Occasionally, when mail arrived, we would receive items from home like gum, Life Savers, and Kool-Aid. In the long journey that the mail had to travel, coupled with the hot, humid climate, there wasn't much that our family could send. The Kool-Aid did a good job of masking the foul tasting water. However, these were pre-pre-sweetened days, and Kool-Aid needed sugar, which at times was a rather scarce commodity. The Life Savers tasted great with all their many flavors, but I soon realized that they had a detrimental effect on my teeth.

We did get a taste of home on one day when the army received some Coke syrup and was doling it out to anyone who wanted it, and I got a whole canteen full. I was unable to use my canteen for anything else for a time, for I had no other container to hold my precious Coke syrup. It didn't require much syrup, only about two spoonfuls to a cup of water. Of course, there was no carbonation and there sure wasn't any ice. To this day, I don't mind if my coke is flat and warm, for I recall how wonderful that warm, flat Coca-Cola tasted to me one time a long time ago.

Many Hollywood stars were putting on shows for the servicemen, but because we were a small group, none of the big names in entertainment ever made an appearance in our area. They performed for groups of tens of thousands.

Some of the local talent did perform for us on a stage that we built in a clearing, with seating on logs laid out in rows.

There was one show, however, that went to more areas and performed more than any other, even putting on their show for small gatherings, and it came to ours—Irving Berlin's, *This Is the Army*. So many of us wanted to see the show that the seating area was roped off and a raffle was held. Although I had one chance in four of getting a seat, I won.

During the show it rained, but we came prepared with our ponchos and nobody left, although they did have to move the band back on the stage out of the rain. Mr. Berlin himself sang, "Oh How I Hate to Get up in the Morning," and then led everyone in singing, "Easter Parade," "White Christmas," and "Alexander's Ragtime Band." I doubt if I'll ever see a more wonderful show, seated on a palm log in the rain on a steamy hot night in a far-away land.

No matter how bad we think we have it, there are always others who have less. It was not the army's responsibility and no government agency was prepared or equipped to feed all the hungry Filipinos. The army's duty was to care for the fighting men, and in the days after the landing, there was scarcely enough for that. Once we were established with some semblance of a camp, the cooks could set up a kitchen tent and prepare what rations they received. We lined up so they could deposit the slop into our mess kits, then we would find a shady spot to sit and eat. The routine when finished eating was to dump the leftovers into the big garbage can, then dip our mess kit into the bucket of hot soapy water, then in the clean hot rinse water, and shake the kit dry before putting it away. Many of the native children, who were street children or orphans dressed in rags, would gather by the big can asking that we dump our leftovers into their outstretched bowl or cup or can. I know that I was not the only one who suffered inwardly from conflicting emotions. I suffered with guilt for not eating all that was on my plate when it appeared that I had so much; guilt for viewing this meal as slop; and also guilt if I ate it all and had nothing left to give. All the while we felt that we were dumping our garbage into a hungry child's outstretched hand. Those sad little eyes were devastating as they tortured our emotions.

We had two cooks in our outfit who seemed to work well together, producing some of our best meals. The pancakes at breakfast time were by far the best any of us had ever tasted. On those mornings that they would be serving pancakes, no one slept late. They were obviously the product of one of the cooks, and it soon became apparent that the other cook was getting a bit jealous with the constant ravings by the men about those pancakes. He finally reached his breaking point one morning when he blurted out, "If you think those pancakes are so damn good, why don't you watch how he prepares them?" Curiosity prompted us to get up a little earlier the next morning so we could see his preparation. He got his great big bowl out, holding it between his knees after filling it with the ingredients and then proceeded to mix it all up by hand. We had seen him washing before he started. But then we noticed to what the other cook must have alluded. He had a wad of chewing tobacco in his cheek and as he mixed the batter, the juices of the tobacco were dripping from the corner of his mouth right into the mixture. From that time on, none of us early morning viewers had pancakes for breakfast. It just might have been that tobacco juice that gave the pancakes that extra good flavor.

Lieutenant McCowan, the commanding officer of our platoon, F Platoon, called me into his tent to tell me that his request to raise me to the rank of corporal had been approved. To a career army man, it would probably have been a time for celebration. But none of us cared what rank we held. We didn't plan to stick around once the war was over. War can make an army of soldiers, disciplined to the rigidity of the chain of command, obliterating the caste system, making everyone equal. It added a couple of dollars at payday, but money was of little use anyway. Much of the time I had been doing the work that according to the army manual was the duty of a sergeant.

The company street consisted of two rows of tents lined up. If this walkway at one time had been grass, it soon became a dry, dusty area from the constant movement of those GI boots coming and going. During combat, while sleeping on the ground, we just threw a blanket over our head at night as protection from weather and bugs; other times it would be a pup tent covering a foxhole. If we had tents in a combat area, they were never aligned, but scattered, hidden under spreading trees or covered with camouflage netting.

When an area was considered secure, tents and cots were provided for a more civilized existence.

This period of April and early May of 1945 was a restful time, a peaceful time, a relaxing time, a busy work time, so different from all the intense hardships that we had experienced since the landing back in October. The heat, on the other hand, was a different story. It was a heat that was extreme, unlike even the Florida summer months when we were on maneuvers. May was hot and dry, so hot that from noon until sunset no work was required and no one ventured from his tent. Even with raised tent flaps to catch a chance breeze, it was just too hot to move. Being close to the equator, the military authorities were well aware of the possible danger from over-exertion by the men at this time of year in such extreme heat. When I ventured out to go to the latrine, there was no one in sight, no movement anywhere. On those hot afternoons we would lie on our cots wearing only our shorts while the sweat poured from our bodies. Even the effort of holding a book to read required too much exertion. A swim in the ocean, so close, would have given a brief respite, even though the water was warm, but the salt coating on our heavily tanned skin would have just caused more discomfort.

After the sun went down the camp would begin to stir. It was a coming alive of a dormant, hibernating army of men. Then there was energy to sit up, to talk, even to get out in that company street and throw a ball.

It was that simple act of throwing the ball that caused the accident. As the sun sank lower and temperature abated, the ball players' energy level increased. Now it was a baseball and a catcher's mitt, throwing faster and harder. "That one was right in there, a strike. Now try a curve ball." Somehow the intended curve went awry. Instead of making it to the catcher, it did curve, but directly under the raised tent flap to where Dymond sat writing a letter home, striking him a terrific blow to his jaw.

When time for leaving the island came, Dymond was still drinking through a straw with his broken jaw wired shut. He could not leave with the rest of the company until the wiring could be removed. Then there would have to be some needed dental work because of his inability to brush his teeth during that long period. I understood the trepidation he felt having us leave him behind, for I had experienced that same scare when I was in the hospital and rumor had our company leaving Leyte. He had been assured that he would eventually catch up to our platoon. A few weeks after our arrival on Okinawa, Dymond did rejoin the company.

"Never volunteer!" a regular army soldier once told me. The meaning of his advice was that if you step forward, you are tempting fate. Volunteering was what I was doing, although actually, I guess, it was more in the way of a choice, rather than volunteering.

The need for our aircraft scanning was no longer required on Leyte, so it was time for us to move on. We had packed all our belongings in our duffel bags and had been trucked down to the docks. Rumors had us moving north to the island of Luzon. Very reluctantly, we boarded the hot, smelly, overcrowded LST, dreading the prospects of spending more days at sea. We mingled around on the deck with little room to even move and no place to sit except on that hard, hot deck. As night came, we spread out, lay down, and slept wherever we could find a place.

In the morning, after hours of hot, miserable waiting, the ship's intercom sounded with the usual, "Attention!" The speaker was reading off a list of names. "Will the following men report to the captain's office?" I had not been listening very intently until I heard my name called as one of those to report. As soon as we were all assembled in the crowded little room, the officer explained the purpose of the summons. He stated simply, "No one has to go, but this is a list of names of the ones chosen to fly ahead of the company to Okinawa." The only option was to wait until this ship was ready to leave and spend the next week at sea. Some of the men stated flatly, "No thanks, I'll wait." Hartzheim, McNicholas, and Sprinkle from our platoon agreed to go. I had never been on an airplane, so I viewed this as my chance to fly, but more importantly, I would not be subjected to those miserable days on that stinking ship on the open ocean. It was really no choice as far as I was concerned. "Yes! Count me in!"

Chapter XIII

Okinawa

Even though we knew we were headed for another dangerous war zone, we were not sorry to be leaving the island of Leyte. So much had happened to us in the months that we had been in the Philippines.

American troops had landed on Okinawa on April first, Easter Sunday. The news we received was that fighting was very intense, and when we left the Philippines in early May, the Japs still held out in the southern part of the island. In addition to the ground fighting, there were constant kamikaze attacks on the fleet that was bringing supplies and reinforcements. Japan viewed this island as their last defense outside of the home islands.

Our scheduled flight called for a stopover on Guam for refueling. Those of us who wanted to go or were willing to go put our duffel bags on our shoulders and left the ship to be trucked out to the airstrip near Tacloban. As expected, there was more delay before the take-off as we stood around in the hot sun. The plane we boarded had long benches on each side with seat belts fastening us to the walls. Then there was more waiting in the close confinement before we finally took off late in the day. With only a few windows, we saw little of the island that had been our home since last October. We landed on Guam in the early morning hours. I had been looking forward to my first plane ride, hoping to see the earth below, but there was nothing for us to see but clouds and dark sky.

Guam was a place that I had read about and been fascinated by, this small island out in the Pacific Ocean that became an American outpost in 1898. Admiral Dewey, on his way to the Philippines when the Spanish-American War began, had stopped at Guam. The Spanish Army contingent stationed there was taken by surprise, because it was unaware that war had been declared between the two countries and they quickly surrendered to the overwhelming odds. Knowing that I would actually be on that island was exciting for me. However, in the brief time that we were on Guam, all I got to see was the small Harmon Air Strip, some old army barracks, and a lot of green. The airstrip was surrounded by forest where everything was green. We crashed on the bunks in the barracks briefly before being roused at 3:00 A.M. to continue our flight.

Radio silence was always maintained once a plane was in the air. On the last leg of our trip, the plan was for us to land on Okinawa on Yontan Air Strip. As we approached Okinawa in the early morning hours, the sun was bright, so we had a bird's view of the island from far above. The strange circular formations we kept seeing below were puzzling. Later we learned that they were burial tombs where the ancestral remains of many Okinawans were stored in big jugs inside those strange-looking stone edifices. Little did we guess at the time that they would be places of refuge for many soldiers during the typhoons that hit the island months later.

Because of the lack of communication, we knew nothing of what was transpiring on the ground while we were in the air.

The Japanese had planned for twelve obsolete bombers, each with a dozen men, to make a suicide strike at the very airfield where we were to land. Four of the planes had mechanical trouble and never took off. The remaining eight took flight but were detected by radar. All were shot down but one before they could accomplish their deadly mission. However, that one escaped the anti-aircraft fire and made a belly landing on Yontan Air Field. The twelve members of the crew, with demolition charges tied around their waists, did considerable damage, managing to destroy twenty-seven planes. When our plane touched down, the grounds crew was clearing the field, bulldozing the remaining burning planes out of the way. This was an entirely different greeting on our arrival on Okinawa than the one we experienced in the Philippine Islands. The battle for this island was an all-out desperate battle and not confined to just the lower portion.

Had we arrived just a little earlier, it's impossible to say what might have happened. After all the many months that we had experienced so many close encounters, we were conditioned to expect the unexpected. Life and death were never very far apart.

Leaving the air field, we boarded several trucks that were to take our group to an area where we could set up camp. We had not gone far on the road, though, when we heard the approach of a flight of planes. As soon as it was determined that they were Zeros, our drivers pulled the trucks to an abrupt stop and while on the run, yelled, "Head for cover!" We jumped from the truck and ran off the road over an embankment into a big ditch and waited. Either we were not observed by the Japs or they were headed for a more important target as they flew past, leaving us to climb back on our trucks and continue on our journey.

Once at the camp site, we set up our two-man pup tents. As Gross had opted for the boat ride, Hartzeim and I joined our tent halves together. Rain began just as we got under cover and continued most of the night.

The next morning the sun was out, and most of us were just emerging from our tents when Hood appeared. His hair matted down, he was wearing only his shorts, was barefooted, and had his rifle in hand. It took several minutes before he could explain his disheveled appearance and what had happened to him and Fontenot. It seems that they had pitched their pup tent in a gulch that had looked like an ideal location—rather secluded, nice grassy spot, shady, and at the same time providing an escape from noise and allowing some protection from possible enemy infiltration.

As they settled in for the night, they had felt secure, comfortable, and dry in their isolated area as the rain began softly hitting the tent.

There are no rivers on Okinawa, but with a heavy downpour, as they were to learn, those seemingly dry gullies during the rainy season fill with water very quickly. The rain begins to accumulate high up in the mountains, gathers momentum, and then cascades down the mountainside, rapidly filling those dry ditches as it races on its way to the ocean.

Late that night, as they peacefully slept, the rain increased, and then very suddenly the water came rushing down into their gully, shocking them awake.

Hood said that when he turned around after reaching high ground and looked back, Fontenot was standing waist deep in the swirling water beside his pup tent with just the tip of the tent's peak showing above the water. He had reached down into the three-foot-deep water and was holding his rifle up in the air as the water ran out of the barrel. Hood said he just stood there surveying this scene, and burst out laughing at Fontenot's sad, dejected appearance and the mess they were in.

Fortunately the water in those gullies recedes almost as quickly as it comes so as soon as it was mostly gone, they were able to gather up their belongings and reset the tent on a higher spot. Since May weather in this climate is rather mild, they were able to dry out quickly.

What had seemed to be a lovely grassy camping ground was certainly not intended for pup tents in the rainy season. Okinawa had appeared so much like terrain at home but was not exactly the same.

It was our ability to laugh at ourselves and our occasional misfortunes that made it possible to cope with our seemingly almost daily challenges.

Three days after we landed, thirty more of our company arrived at Yomtan Air Strip. Our company supply officer was able to obtain a squad tent for our group, complete with wooden floor, where we could spread out our blankets. Then the following week, we moved into six-man pyramidal tents without the wooden flooring. There was that old choice—the soft ground close to nature and all its crawling critters or the hard, inflexible wood flooring.

One fellow in our tent came up with an idea for heating our rations and water for coffee. The stove, using the term loosely, consisted of a can from the C-rations filled with sand and gasoline and set into the ground. We had to close our tent up tightly so as not to show any light that might give guidance to an enemy plane. This gave us one small pleasure to look forward to at the end of the day. The coffee, sugar, and cream we acquired deviously by finding a loose edge to the cook tent. We hadn't commandeered much, but it soon became obvious that we were not the only ones. Word was sent out that the items missing from the cook tent were to be returned or else! The "or else" was to be a tent-by-tent inspection to recoup the stolen goods. As the six of us had so enjoyed our evening cup of coffee, we were determined not to part with those things willingly. Apparently there were others in the company who were of the same mind-set, as none of the items were returned. This made it necessary for the officers to do their threatened thorough tent-by-tent search. What we needed was a good hiding place for our ill-gotten goods. When the inspection team reached our tent, they methodically searched the whole tent, moved our equipment and belongings, looked under our blankets, and even searched in our duffel bags. But they neglected to look inside our GI five-gallon water can where we had sealed our treasure in watertight packages. If the officers had lifted the lid of that water can, they still would not have seen our prized goods beneath the water. Our evening coffee ritual, though not served in a china cup with saucer but in our metal mess kit cup, was still one small pleasure that we could continue to anticipate.

The evening when it was my turn to light our little stove, I slipped out as usual and tapped off a small tin can full of gasoline from the company generator. Casually, I poured the gas into the can, which already contained the sand from the previous night. Then, being in no rush, I closed the tent flaps and filled the big can with water to be placed over the fire. Only after all this preparation did I strike the match.

In one great swoosh, the flames shot out in all directions, burning my bare feet and singing all the hair from my legs. It was all over with just that one big burst. The others in the tent, for a few seconds, were stunned silent before they began laughing at my impromptu dance. What I learned that day was gasoline does not burn, but the fumes sure do.

For best reception radar units were always placed at a high point where they could receive the best signals. In June our platoon was re-assigned to the top of a mountain, the highest point on the island of Okinawa. When we finally reached the top, we were greeted with what sounded like, "No room at the Inn." Our lieutenant had been informed that we would receive support from the Marines already located there. Yet when we got there after our arduous, four-hour drive, we found that the Marines had encircled the mountain top area with many enclosures of barbed wire and land mines and had posted guards at close intervals. We were not allowed to enter their sanctum.

Access to this mountain peak was along a narrow, winding road built for animal trails. The steep sides had sheer drops of hundreds of feet. The road was so narrow that in some places, as we rounded a curve, the left side of the truck would be scraping the rock wall while one wheel of the truck would be hanging free with only three of the wheels touching the road. As the front right wheel again resumed its place on the road, the rear right wheel would be hanging out in space. We crowded over to the left side of the truck, not daring to even look down.

At the beginning of this long, difficult climb, before it became so steep, the road was a gradual incline, wet and muddy with deep ruts. The driver of our three-quarter-ton truck was having a difficult time keeping the truck moving forward as we rocked from side to side when suddenly it slid off the muddy roadway, over the edge, and set us into a very precarious predicament. For a time we dared not move, fearing that the slightest movement might roll our suspended truck over. Carefully we shifted our weight to the high side of the truck and then taking turns, one at a time, we climbed out. With a lot of sweat and strain, we managed to get the truck back onto the road.

From some of the Marines at our final destination we learned why they had all the excessive precautions. According to the information they had received, four Jap soldiers had been assigned a suicide mission with the single purpose of putting this particular Marine company out of action. It was when one of the four was captured and two were killed that they learned of this plot. With the one remaining Jap still unaccounted for and willing and eager to sacrifice himself, it is understandable that the Marines were somewhat paranoid. They stated flatly that there was just no room for our platoon within their enclosure.

We set up our tents outside this impregnable fortress, taking proper precautions, and posting a twenty-four-hour guard for our few tents while we awaited further instructions. From this mountaintop we had an absolutely spectacular view. At this site on Okinawa we were away from all of war's devastation. Living daily in an environment where all that man and nature have created has been damaged or completely destroyed has a very detrimental effect on morale. On that mountaintop we could admire the beauty of the hills and green all around.

As we were unable to erect our radar set at the peak, according to our instructions, we waited. This gave us some free time to explore the area.

Dymond, Gross, Hartzeim, and I set out exploring the hillside. We found a path on the other side of the mountain from the roadway and started out hiking and stumbling down the side of the mountain. We followed a small, narrow dirt path that was the only thing that was not green. Tall trees stood out along the way with all of the ground covered with various types of plants and grasses. From where we could look out across the island, the waves of green covered hills, valleys, and rises gave the impression of ocean swells. As we rounded one curve on the path, we came upon a small waterfall. The water was running from a spring about eight feet up and was coming over a rock ledge right onto another flat ledge. Here was nature's most perfect natural shower stall with only the shower curtain missing. However, with no neighbors in sight, it really wasn't a necessity. In the past weeks there had been few opportunities for us to get a complete wash. We stood there for a while looking out at the great expanse, with no disruptions of natural vegetation. Then we looked at the waterfall we'd found, looked at each other, and then with one thought in mind—*let's do it!*—one of the guys ran back up the hill to our camp for soap and towels and one by one, we got under the icy water while the others stood guard. Being naked out in territory where there was suspected enemy nearby tends to make one a bit nervous. The lack of clothing, should an enemy appear, would detract from one's military stance, even though the rifle, propped against a rock nearby, could be quickly retrieved. For men who were resigned to wearing and sleeping in the same dirty clothing day after day, this ice cold shower was a great lift to our spirits.

Three days later orders came for our platoon to return to the foot of the mountain to be shipped out to Tori Shima, a coral rock in the China Sea, fifty miles west of Okinawa. We were to be the most forward post, giving early aircraft warning.

There would also be a small Marine unit on Tori Shima. Though our island was small (approximately 150 feet by 1,500 feet), we were willing to share it with those Marines.

Chapter XIV

Tori Shima

For the nine weeks that we spent on Tori Shima, we were awarded a unit citation for isolation duty. However, like so many of war's contradictions, it was more a period of insulation than isolation. We were removed from all of war's filth, death, and destruction on Okinawa.

As a radar unit giving early warning of aircraft activity, Tori Shima was a logical site. It is situated fifty miles due west of Okinawa and just five miles from Kume Shima, an island still held by the Japs. Though the word *shima* in Japanese means "island," Tori was not what could be considered an island, but rather a large chunk of coral, completely devoid of any vegetation, protruding from the sea, measuring approximately 1,500 feet long and 150 feet wide, and varying in height, at places rising to eighty feet. We were placed out in the China Sea closer to Japan than any other unit.

Our company, the 727 SAW Co. (signal aircraft warning) comprised six platoons—A through F, with each platoon consisting of approximately thirty men. But only A platoon and our F platoon were to be stationed on Tori.

June 9 we were loaded on an LSM (landing ship medium). No vehicles could possibly navigate the peculiar coral terrain, so the big open area on the LSM contained all our equipment and supplies. The first night we slept on the ship, lying on our duffel bags. In the morning we set sail for Tori Shima. On this boat was a detachment of twenty-five to thirty Marines to also be stationed on our island. They had in their possession, briefly, one whole canned chicken. It was "briefly" as some one in our air corps group swiped it. That, too, was brief as it was quickly retrieved. For a time, it looked as though there might be an inter-service war over that canned chicken before the officers interceded. Living on hard biscuits and canned hash turned a chicken (canned or otherwise) into an epicurean delight. Unfortunately I never got a chance to taste it, but I'm still convinced that it would have been the best-tasting chicken ever.

Squawking gooney birds, like dive bombers, greeted us when we landed. They would swoop down on us and let go their loads, seldom missing their targets. That was the way it

Tori Shima

started and during our stay, they never let up. Those gooney birds were actually a common sea bird, probably of the tern family, but we were really not at all interested in learning more about our fellow occupants of that coral rock. Those pesky birds considered this spot their private home. For generations they had laid their eggs and raised their young, undisturbed by man. To them we were interlopers. They told us and showed us in many ways every day that we were just not wanted. Their instincts had them protecting their nests at all cost. It seemed as if they knew instinctively that we recoiled from the excrement they rained down on us. We had learned very early the necessity of always covering our heads. No man ever got away without being hit by a splat. But when their bomb landed in one's mess kit, it had the effect of ending that meal with complete loss of appetite. We went about our daily chores, attempting to avoid any proximity to their nests. Since there were so many nests on the island scattered throughout the crevasses, it was not possible to dodge those birds.

Because of the size and shape of Tori Shima, it was often mistaken, especially at night, for a warship. On more than one occasion, we were torpedoed by a passing ship that mistook us for an enemy vessel. Our indestructible coral ship, Tori, not only did not sink, but its occupants had their sleep disturbed only briefly.

Our tents were set on different levels depending on where we could find or chisel out a level spot. The tents were then covered with camouflage netting so that to the occasional observer, the island appeared uninhabited. Even the sea birds that flew above us kept us hidden. On our coral rock, we were away from all the waste and constant sounds of war that we had left on Okinawa. We heard only the never-ending squawking of those gulls.

On Okinawa there was little of what man had created that was not damaged or completely demolished. Living with that havoc day after day was depressing. Destruction was everywhere. Nothing was left undamaged and so much was completely destroyed. It was difficult to exist in surroundings of so much destruction. One's thoughts tended to dwell on the labor that mankind had expended in creating things, which now all lay in rubble. Nowhere was there an unsacred building. Entire housing areas were erased. One picture I still carry in my memory is of a bare wasteland, the earth scorched, no trees left whole, with one building still standing in the middle of that desolate area—a small church, damaged but defiant.

There were no trees or vegetation of any kind on Tori and no water except for what rainwater collected in small indentations. If it did not rain for several days, those puddles became stagnant, foul-smelling mosquito breeding pools. Although we were not bothered by mosquitoes because of the ever-present wind, that stench could, at times, become overwhelming.

I busied myself one day filling in an indentation that contained a stinking pool just outside our tent. By chipping and pounding at the coral, I created a material to fill in and level off the area to keep water from collecting.

Our drinking water was desalinated salt water pumped from the ocean surrounding us. In the salt removal process, the water was stored in open, cylindrical fifteen-foot diameter tanks before it was placed in canvas bags. My family sent me some Kool-Aid which I mixed in the water to change the taste. I often wondered if the lousy taste came from the hot canvas bags or perhaps from a passing bird.

The only indication that man had ever been there was an area where our boats docked. It appeared that probably Japanese fishermen had built a landing place by chipping away some of the coral to form a flat area.

There were many places on this earth that we would rather have been, but on the whole, compared to where we had been and what we had endured, it was easy, peaceful, and almost pleasant. There was very little for us to do when we finished our shift operating the radar set and sending routine messages to headquarters on Okinawa. Out on that rock there wasn't even a need for guards. Much of our leisure time was spent as before, playing cards, reading, or writing letters. Except for the squawking birds, it was a very quiet place. There were periods of casual walks along the shore, picking up shells or skimming chunks of coral over the water.

When the tide was at its lowest, the island more than doubled in size, forming a big shelf on which one could walk out. In the cracks in the coral on that shelf were many and varied types of tropical fish of all sizes, shapes, and colors. The contents of a fish tank in the dentist's waiting room back in the civilized world would have cost thousands of dollars if filled with what swam about in the water in those cracks. Those little swimmers could have made us rich if only we had a way to ship them home.

For increased early warning, each of our two platoons was given a second radar set, and I was put in charge of our second one, responsible for its operation. It was my duty to arrange my crew, rotating the men to cover the twenty-four-hour operation and be fair to all. If any man was not able for any reason to work his hours, I filled in for him. During the war every radar set was given a code name, and my unit was named "Scarlet."

Each four-hour shift on the radar consisted of two men. Most of the time one man could handle the job, just turning the antenna and watching the scope. If any action was detected, it would require that one man track while the other maintain radio contact with headquarters. Only once did I spread my blanket on the ground to lie down and rest while my partner was watching the radar screen. The bird lice may have been small, but they sure could bite.

Supplies and food would arrive every other week by boat from Okinawa. Among those supplies were new GI boots. Our army boots were made of top-grade, thick leather and were ankle-high, providing us with good protection for wherever we traveled. We had thought them to be indestructible but, tough as they were, they were no match for that coral. Its sharp edges chewed away at the leather with every step.

Our food was the same old dehydrated, monotonous fare. With so many birds close at hand, we concluded one day that those antagonists just might possibly become a nice supplement to our diet. There would not be much meat on each bird, but still it would present a change. Any change, we thought, would be better than dehydrated, reconstituted "guess what." For men with little variety and short food supply, those flying bombers presented the prospect of real food. Not being very alert fowl, it was easy for us to sneak up on them from below, reach over a coral projection, and grab them. My family had at one time raised chickens, so as I was experienced in plucking and preparing fowl, I got the duty of getting the birds ready for cooking. There was a great deal of discussion as to exactly how to cook them, but there was really a very limited choice.

As we watched those rare delicacies boil in an open pot over the fire, visions of sweet, tender meat stirred our taste buds and as they slowly cooked, anticipation tended, at least in our minds, to enhance the very flavor of that soon to be eaten treat. When finally each man got his piece of meat, as it went into his mouth, he looked stunned. For a few moments, we looked at each other and then it came, the spitting out of what we had been so anticipating. Fish—rotten-tasting, second-hand fish! We had forgotten that oft-quoted line, "you are what you

73

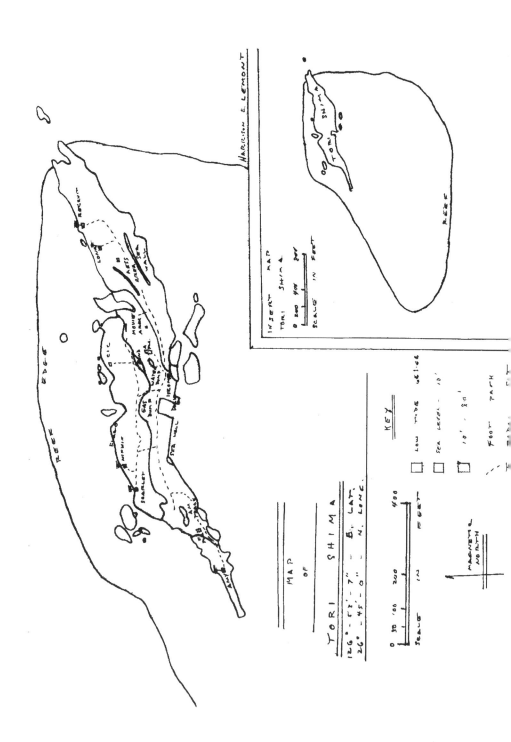

MAP
OF
TORI SHIMA
126° - 51' - 7" - E. LAT.
26° - 45' - 0" - N. LONG.

SCALE IN FEET
0   50   100   200   400

MAGNETIC
AND NORTH

KEY

□   LOW TIDE HEDGE
□   SEA LEVEL - 10'
□   10' - 20'
      FOOT PATH

INSERT MAP
TORI SHIMA

SCALE IN FEET
0 200 400 600

HARRISON E. LEMONT

74

eat," and that must also apply to gooney birds. They were obviously not corn-fed chicks.

But what about the eggs? It had been a long time since we had viewed the sight of fried eggs with their golden crowns encircled by pure white borders, bubbling and sputtering in a pan. We were very careful to empty a nest to be sure that the eggs were fresh. But like the birds themselves, they were not eggs, they, too, were second-hand fish!

Periodically a Piper Cub would fly in from Okinawa bringing us news and mail. It was a time of anticipation—a letter from home. The plane would come in at the broad side of the island assuming that it was as wide as it was long. Yet in spite of our jumping up and down, shouting, "Drop the bag; let it go!" they seldom dropped it soon enough, delivering our mail out where some good swimmer had to swim frantically to retrieve it before it sank below the waves.

One evening one of our own planes decided to practice his machine gun fire on our coral rock down there. I guess no one had told him we were down here; our camouflaging was just too good. Though it did startle us, no one was hurt and no damage was done. The pilot continued flying on, completely unaware of our presence.

With so much free time, one day I decided to map the island. With paper and colored pencils and not much else, I set out pacing off distances and estimating heights. I indicated on the map the dimensions, physical shapes, and locations of each tent, the radar sets, the cooking area, and the latrines; and by using color, showed the different elevations. I spent a lot of time pacing off distances and marking my calculations on a rough draft.

At one end of our cigar-shaped rock, the water was very calm and, therefore, I could walk up to the water's edge with no problem. But at the other end, the waves were continually crashing over that point. Since it was very slippery, it was dangerous and difficult for me to get true measurements as I climbed over the rocks. Sitting out there as I wrote on my pad of paper it felt as if the ocean waves were crashing over the bow of our coral ship. I could understand how we could easily be mistaken in the dark for a passing vessel. My tent mates followed my progress as I worked on my map and each in turn asked me if I would make a copy for them. I was flattered that they wanted a copy and there was plenty of time to make reproductions. When our company captain saw the copy I had made for our platoon lieutenant, he asked me for four copies of the map. My map was to become a part of the written history of our company.

On that day, the fifteenth of August 1945, word of war's end reached us out on that rock. Back home, the headlines would read "Japan Surrenders," but we waited, afraid to believe it could be true. Could the war really be over, this war that we thought would not end until we landed on the Japanese main islands and fought mile by mile and year by year, until every Jap had jumped off the other end? This Pacific War had been that way with so many previous battles, hopping from one island to the next. For the Japanese, death was preferable to surrender. Could a true miracle have occurred? Were we going home? We dared not even think *home for Christmas.*

We heard rumors of some GIs on Okinawa getting shot by others in their own outfit, celebrating. For us, it was a calm, reflective period, with trepidations—joy tempered with fear that it might not be true. We talked of the past and about resuming our interrupted lives. The war we had thought would never end had suddenly, abruptly stopped. The next few weeks, though, were no different from the previous ones. We continued operating our radar sets, but in a more relaxed mood.

All during the war, we received only scattered bits of information about the progress of our war. We knew that our aircraft had been bombing the Japanese homeland on a regular daily run from Okinawa. We heard one day of one huge bomb being dropped on Japan. I figured, what does it matter, a planeload of bombs or one big one? We only learned later of America's new weapon and how much havoc that one bomb could cause. Terrible as it was, without that atomic bomb, how much longer would the war have continued? How many more American lives would have been lost? And how many Japanese lives were saved by forcing Japan to surrender?

On the day that the Japanese declared for peace, a flight of planes was making its routine trip to bomb what was left of Tokyo. With this news of surrender, the planes were ordered to return. Because of the risk of landing a plane loaded with bombs, they were instructed to eject them into the ocean. However, the pilots figured as long as they had to drop their bombs, why not try to see if they could hit that coral formation? Fortunately for us, those bombers weren't any better at hitting us than were the Piper Cubs with the mailbags.

Eventually a boat came to pick us up with all our equipment. We cleaned up the area, packed all our things, and left the place as we had found it. We were conditioned to following orders without knowing where we were going, but on the boat ride back to Okinawa, we knew that from this point on our destiny had dramatically changed. This was the first ride on our way home.

They won—the rock's only other inhabitants, those gooney birds that resented our presence! We had tolerated each other, we and those birds, and now the time had come for us to leave. We were as glad to be going as they were to have us go. But the flapping of their wings as our boat pulled away—were they waving?

Chapter XV

The Long, Long Wait

War's end saw very few changes for us, except for the food. We began getting some fresh meat and even iced drinks. As the surrender signing was set to take place in Tokyo Harbor aboard the *USS Missouri*, we felt that that date would bring a big change. Nothing changed! It was hard to believe that the war was over. President Truman announced, "All servicemen will be home as soon as transports can carry them." But where were all those ships?

We began seeing movies almost every night. A short film at the show one night was titled *Three Down and No Transports*. It was a spoof on the film *Two Down and One to Go*, which was a movie shown just after V-E Day, the end of the war with Germany and Italy.

Based on years of service, age, time overseas, time in combat, marriage, children, etc., each of us received a priority number. It was considered the fairest way to decide the order in which each serviceman would be returned to the States. Those who had suffered the most or were most needed at home would be the first to leave. I had fifty-six points, which was average for our company. The first group, about sixty, to leave our company, were men over thirty-eight years of age and with eighty-five points. Schweibert, who was thirty-nine years old and considered old compared to the rest of us, had priority for age but didn't have the required number of points. Ever since our time at Ormoc I had been doing the job of sergeant and was promised that rank as soon as there was a vacancy. As Schweibert held that rank, I was almost as anxious for him to leave as he was. Although rank was never very important to any of us, it still would have been nice to receive the recognition.

Stuck with another long waiting period, Gross and I set out to see some of the island, hitching a ride first to Naha, the capital. It was, or had been, a much larger and more modern city than Ormoc but just as desolate. We saw the railroad station, university, theater, prison, some department stores, and the docks, but rarely was there a building with even two walls still standing. From there we hitched a ride to Shuri, which is where I saw that defiant chapel still standing although all around it was completely flattened. The whole area was as flat as if it had been stepped on by a giant.

To keep busy, one afternoon Ogden and I did some repair work on the road that ran into our camp. I even volunteered to help unload supplies and helped the cooks clean up after a meal.

It was a generally restless, almost desperate need to keep busy feeling that permeated the whole camp. We were waiting now to get started building our new life, a whole life that lay ahead, if only our ship would arrive. Before this, we had been complacent, just living day to day, performing our duties. Now every day had meaning.

After the peace treaty signing on September 3rd, we'd figured things would change. They did! But not as we had thought or hoped. We left headquarters area at Kadena to relocate eighteen miles away at the end of Katchin Hanto peninsula on a steep cliff overlooking Buckner Bay. In this new location, we were to commence radar operation again.

In August I received a letter from my brother, Bob. He spoke of what he had been doing and that his ship, the *Euryale*, would be headed for Japan with a scheduled stop at Okinawa on September 20. Excitedly, I wrote to his fleet post office address, telling him that I was on Okinawa. What a break this would be from the waiting and what a thrill, if all went well, to get to see a member of my own family.

Censorship for all servicemen started when they first received that APO or FPO address. All correspondence was carefully scrutinized. It was not possible for anyone to know where any serviceman was located. The censors were merciless with their knives and scissors, cutting out anything they deemed even slightly questionable. With war's end, being able to write openly, saying whatever we wished, giving facts, locations, telling all, was something we could not have imagined just weeks earlier. Until that letter arrived, neither of us knew where the other one was, only that he was in the navy on a ship and I was with the Army Air Corps somewhere in the Pacific.

From his letter, I learned that his ship was docked in Perth, Australia, where their duty was to service submarines needing repairs. With war's end, their services would be required at a base in Japan.

It was a three-quarter-hour ride from camp down to the shore where Gross and I went to see the port master. It would still be weeks before Bob's ship was due to arrive, but we were just seeking information as we went from dock to dock. We wanted to find out where the *Euryale* would anchor and where the small craft would bring men ashore. Buckner Bay was crowded with ships of all sizes. When we eventually found the man who had the schedule of ship arrivals and departures, he had not yet received any information on the one about which we were inquiring.

Every day, I hitched a ride to the beach area; and every day to my question, that man with the clipboard in hand just replied, "Not yet."

In camp, we received word of an impending storm headed for Okinawa. As a precaution, the radar tent and equipment were taken down and stored in a nearby cave. We tied our tent securely with extra ropes at all corners and felt quite complacent. As the winds and rain began early in the morning, the kitchen tent blew down. By noon, as the storm intensified, the squad tent collapsed. As for the six of us, there was nothing to do but lie on our cots and wait it out. The wind and rain kept increasing in intensity, pelting our canvas covering, yet in spite of the whipping rain and wind, our structure held. By morning it was the only one still standing.

The island's natives, from years of experience, knew well what these all-too-frequent typhoons could do. Their houses were built behind high walls with sturdy, rugged, stunted trees for extra protection. The US Army, with bulldozers and other earth-moving equipment, had cleared away much of the natural barriers to the fury of the winds.

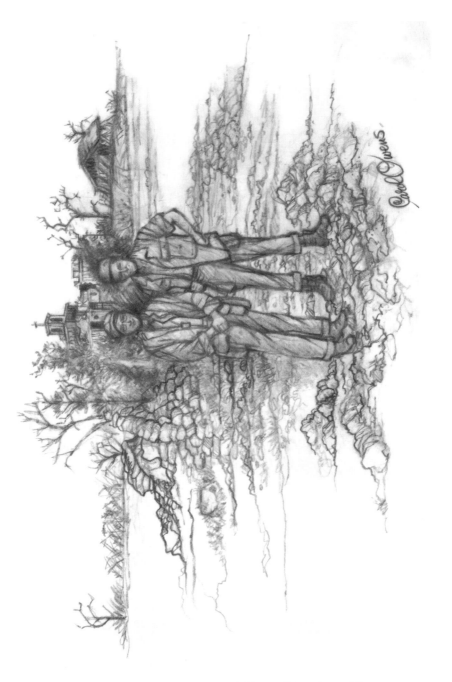

Schweibert and Lemont in front of Shuri Chapel on Okinawa

Near our camp was an underground emplacement built into the hill by the Japs. It had cement walls and a wooden ceiling and was hidden with a grass covering. It was about 100 feet long with an opening at each end. In the middle was a ten feet by ten feet area for gun sights with narrow openings on the ocean side. It was intended as a defensive position where guns had once been mounted by the Japs.

Our pyramidal tent was a four-sided affair with four chains, one from each corner, fastening the canvas enclosure to the spike that protruded from the top of the center pole. A small canvas cap fit over that spike to make a nice tight seal. On each side of the entrance, which was a flap-covered opening, we had a cot, then one on each side wall and then two in the back. It provided comfortable space for the six of us—Gross, Dymond, Hartzeim, Odell, Schweibert, and me. From salvaged lumber, we had built a platform and a circular table in the middle of the tent that wrapped around the center pole. It was a good place for writing letters, reading, or playing cards.

When this first typhoon of the season subsided, our tent looked tattered and frayed, but it was still upright. We had a great deal of work to do cleaning up the area and re-setting our radar unit in order to operate again. We helped some other guys resurrect their old tents or replacement tents. We seemed to be back to normal rather quickly. However, we sensed that our tents, like all the rest of the army tents and equipment, being out in the open, were easy targets for the next wind.

On that stormy day, I lost some of my belongings, but what was worse for me was the storm put Buckner Bay out of operation, resulting a great deal of damage at the shore and destroying the docks. With it, I lost my source of information on ship movements.

When September 20 arrived, I was off again, headed for the port master, as that was the day the *Euryale* was scheduled to arrive. By the time I reached Brown Beach, I was too late to catch the ferry out to his ship. At this exact same time, Bob was arriving at the headquarters of my company. By the time he found it, it was too late in the day for him to proceed farther to where our platoon was camped.

The following day, our company headquarters sent me a note that Bob had been there on his quest to find me. The message I received said simply, "I'll be looking for you." Pondering the wording of his note, it seemed to me that it could be taken either way. I chose the wrong interpretation and waited. So did he, waiting for my arrival.

The next day, no more waiting! I secured a pass and left camp, headed again for the docks. My pass was good until 6:00 P.M. By 1:30 I caught the small landing craft that ferried men around to the various ships in the bay, reaching his ship at 3:00 only to discover that he had left. It was at that same hour that he had finally reached my camp. The last boat to leave his ship in the evening would be the one I would be disembarking from and the one he would have to board to get back to his ship.

Word came down from the ship's captain that all visitors were to leave the ship on that last ferry of the day. Determined not to miss him again and with his shipmate's help, I was moved from one hiding place to another to avoid the ship's SPs, who were searching for me. When the small craft left without me, they had to keep me overnight, but it was understood that I was to leave on the launch at 7:00 in the morning. When Bob reached the ship, he had with him a pass from my officer extending my leave time. My lieutenant was aware of our frustrated attempts to get together and suspected that I wouldn't be back to camp that night, but he didn't want any of his men to be AWOL. A friend of Bob's gave up his bunk near my brother's, and we talked most of the night. It had been three years since we had seen each other.

The following day, Bob arrived at my camp so I could reciprocate, showing him all around my world just as he had given me the tour of his ship. He brought with him a shoe box full of apples and oranges. Fresh fruit was a rare delicacy that my buddies gratefully devoured. But beyond that, he also brought with his presence, a sense of that other life that had no equivalent in this one. To meet with a member of one's own family in this chaotic world on the other side of the globe was just not possible. But it happened.

When time came for him to get back to his ship, I loaded him up with Jap souvenirs, cards, and papers but also with some K-rations so he could get a sense of our diet. We planned to get together again the next day.

Early in the morning I got down to Brown Beach. The first boat from his ship would leave at 7:00, reaching the beach at 7:45. I wanted to be sure to catch that boat. But the harbor looked strangely different that morning. Many of the biggest ships were missing. The port master said they were forecasting another typhoon due to hit Okinawa soon.

His ship was gone!

Chapter XVI

Typhoon

All our concerns about our long wait for the ship that would carry us home were suspended on October 9 when a second typhoon hit Okinawa. The forecast predicted a more intense storm, and right from the beginning we sensed that this one would be much tougher. The winds were stronger than before, and the rain seemed to be coming down harder and from all directions. We were concerned about our tent as it was beginning to leak in places where the canvas showed the strains from the previous storm, but we felt secure. Actually I guess one could say that we were somewhat cocky, having had the only tent to withstand that other typhoon. The noise of wind and rain was so loud that we could only communicate by shouting, so we just sat or lay on our cots. There was nothing for us to do but wait it out.

Gross lifted the flap to have a look at what was happening and was literally blown back inside. It was impossible to tell what was happening outside the tent. The winds kept getting stronger as time passed, whipping all around the tent in a howling gale.

We just looked at each other. It was not possible to be heard above the noise that the wind was making because it kept getting stronger and louder. We could only nervously sit and wait.

The increased intensity of the rain that was beating on the canvas caused water to leak in at the seams in several places. We kept moving our personal belongings around to keep them from getting wet. It didn't make much difference where we set our things, but it gave us something to do.

Sitting there listening to the howling wind as it intensified and watching the tent trembling, we began to wonder if it was going to hold. We had an eerie feeling that something was about to happen, when suddenly one of the chains at the peak snapped, allowing the tent to sag on that side, creating a very precarious situation. Dymond quickly jumped up on our table, trying desperately to grab the loose chain as it whipped about. I had a piece of wire that I was ready to hand to him, if only he could catch that chain. The rest of the guys braced themselves against that side of the tent to hold it up and lessen the strain so Dymond could catch it and somehow secure it. But the three remaining chains could no longer hold the tent against the strong wind and as each chain broke loose, the whole tent collapsed. Instead of just lying flat on top of us, though, the erratic wind caused our flattened tent to begin beating up and down. When we had built our table in the center of the tent, we could not have guessed the part it would later play in our safety. As the tent with its loose chains whipped about, some of us huddled under that table while others crawled under their cots to avoid those beating chains. The table was being splintered by that metal whip as our canvas covering kept rising and falling and ripping apart. With what opportunity the rising and falling of the tent permitted, we started creeping out the opening when suddenly our shredded tent was gone, along with most of our cots and personal things.

As the wind lessened and then intensified, we crawled toward the old Jap tunnel. The wind was so strong that we had to crawl and then periodically lie flat holding on to whatever we could grab on to, a tree trunk or bush. It looked as if everything was blowing away. I saw our metal antenna crate fly over the cliff. Empty fifty-five-gallon drums were flying through the air like leaves from a tree. Our cots flew past us down the cliff. So much was flying or rolling by that we could not tell what was happening. It was almost impossible to see anything with the blinding rain. We moved by instinct, headed for that underground protection.

Finally safe from the wind inside the tunnel, we milled about, damp and cold and we stood in puddles of water. The wooden ceiling was leaking in many places, continually dripping on us. Our officer was trying to create some order out of all the chaos. Looking about, I realized that Gross was not there. Without thinking, but rather by instinct, I ran out looking for him. I found him trying to salvage some of his personal belongings. "Leave them!" I shouted, but with the roaring wind, he couldn't hear me. Together we managed to drag what we could into the safety of the cave. In an event of this magnitude, you realize how important the other guy is to you.

Later we learned that many men in other areas were forced to seek shelter inside the native tombs that are scattered around the island. They had to squeeze in among the many burial jugs of Okinawans' ancestral bones, a weird haven from the storm. It made us realize how fortunate we were that this tunnel-cave was so close to our camp, providing us a refuge.

With dawn, the sun was out bright and all was calm again. Looking up at the clear blue sky, one could almost believe that nothing had happened. Although the typhoon had passed, in its wake it left destruction in every direction.

It was an unbelievable sight. All the docks that had been visible from our lofty perch, protruding from the land like so many fingers reaching out into Buckner Bay, were gone. Not one dock was in sight anywhere, washed away with the wind and waves. Many small ships as well as one big seaplane had been tossed up on the shore. The quonset huts below us on the dock side were only skeletons. The sheets of metal that had once securely wrapped those buildings had been torn from their rivets and sent sailing away like tissue paper kites. Our view in the other direction where the army was in the process of building gasoline storage tanks was only flattened metal scrap. The big lumberyard located near the tanks had the appearance of a giant's box of toothpicks spilled across the landscape. The Seabee base just down the slope below us had been covered by a huge mudslide, leaving only bits of tents, cots, and other paraphernalia protruding from the mud where once there had been a camp.

No attempt was made by the Seabees to salvage what was left of their camp buried under all that mud. However, many items that were abandoned by them allowed us to rebuild our camp better than before. In the process, we were able to find many usable items in that former Seabee base. Among the things I dug out of the mud were two bed sheets in perfect condition. Cleaning those sheets in my helmet, though difficult and time consuming, was a labor of love. I slept in sheer luxury, for no one had anything of greater value to get me to trade away those sheets.

War's destruction, it seems, though devastating causes no more damage than what nature can do.

Chapter XVII

Mouse Trap

Though the war was over, it was hard to tell, since our life went on with each day just the same as the one before, except for a different shift-time operating the radar. Almost every night they were showing a movie at the base just down the hill from us. We piled into the back of our truck and made the bumpy ride down the straight, steep road to the lower level. Then it was a U-turn on the graveled road to follow the coastal trail, past those quonset huts below our camp, to the area where they had set up the screen. The whole trip took one hour to get down to that site, but it was well worth it to be able to see and do something different. If we had opted to go directly down from our camp on the cliff, it would probably have taken about five minutes. But then there would have undoubtedly been many bruises and no way back.

The food that we were getting was much better, almost good. And there was even some variety. From our lofty spot, we could sit on the edge of the cliff and watch the ships in Buckner Bay as they maneuvered, some arriving and some leaving. But as it appeared to us, there was not as much activity as we would liked to have seen. It could be very depressing to watch and wonder, as the days ticked by. Home for Christmas, for some strange reason, seemed to be a deadline, but as each day passed, chances of getting there by that date grew slimmer. It never occurred to me that my buddy, Gross, may not have felt the same way, for we never spoke openly of what might affect us beyond our daily routine. His thoughts may have been of Hanukkah.

Schweibert left on September 30, which meant I was eligible for sergeant rating, but then I learned that there is a therty-day waiting period after one man leaves an outfit before another is allowed his rating. So I didn't get the sergeant stripes, but I much preferred home anyway. However, I had to take over the operation of his crew, which consisted of Hurford, Willenborg, Hood, and Fontenot.

The weather on Okinawa in late spring was mild, much like New England, but minus the mosquitoes. What a contrast it was with the Philippines, where we had always slept with netting over us. Poles fastened to each end of our cots supported the netting above us. It had become a nightly ritual, climbing into bed and then adjusting our screen covering and killing the one or two that got in with us. What a relief it was to lie down without the pests or the chore and fuss with the mosquito net.

When we erected our six-man pyramidal tent, we built a firm, wooden support along the sides to give more rigidity to the structure, and we also built a wood flooring. It took a lot of scrounging to get the wood and nails, but it gave our home an element of stability—not luxurious, but somewhat comfortable. Each time we moved, the same six of us got together. After erecting our tent, we would do what we could with the materials we gathered to make our temporary home livable. After so many moves, we got quite good at knowing exactly what we wanted and how to do it. We spent little time in our tent, though, as we were operating our radar unit twenty-four hours every day. Even though the war, theoretically, was over, it sure didn't seem that way. We still had to be constantly alert. We could not be sure that the Japs would honor the cease-fire agreement. We were warned that there might still be enemy troops hiding or some that had not received word of the end of hostilities. These scattered few could be dangerous fanatics.

Our nights were rather uneventful, until Finnigan claimed one morning that he'd been bitten during the night. "Look, right there on my hand," he kept saying, but no one was showing much concern.

A few nights later, Odell claimed a mouse ran over his bed. We laughed, joking that, "You're seeing shadows, or it's just your imagination."

Then, when I awoke one night to find a mouse sitting right on my forehead, never before or since have I moved so quickly from the prone to the upright position, so fast that my movement propelled that critter to the far side of the tent where it disappeared.

It was this series of events that prompted us to set a mouse trap, foolishly thinking we could solve the problem of the island's rodent population. But at the same time, we very wisely resurrected our old netting and henceforth spent every night under that covering. Maybe there wasn't a mosquito problem to concern us, but we sure didn't care for the rodent traffic.

In the morning, the mouse trap we had set had been sprung and there was blood on it, so obviously the creature was injured, even though it got away.

Several weeks later we detected a strange odor in the tent, but we assumed it was just a passing phase as there were many strange smells around. But the next day, the odor was stronger and getting down right unpleasant and obviously it was in our tent. We saw no visible signs of any decaying matter around. We searched under all the bunks, moved all our belongings, but found nothing. Another day and the odor was even worse, but now we were able to isolate it. It was coming from the back, in one corner of the tent. We had to move a couple of the bunks and rip up some of the floorboards, but there it was—a dead rat! We had not made the connection between the smell and the trap that we had set some time before. We may not have killed a mouse, but we had mortally wounded a rat.

He didn't get away after all! But that wasn't true of the rest of his relatives. A couple of days later, as we were reading or writing, a mouse nonchalantly strolled through our tent. Everyone grabbed a club of some kind and made swings at him. He just ducked under this or over that and disappeared. I'm sure I heard him laughing. Okinawa was so overrun with rodents, I guessed that was why we got plague shots before we left Leyte.

As some men got their notice to move to a holding area, the first step in the procedure of returning, others were brought in to replace them. On my crew, Philips and Blasawich replaced Hurford and Willenborg; and when Odell and Schweibert left for the waiting area, Thomas and Finnegan took their place in our tent.

On November 6, we took down our old radar, left Katchen Hanto peninsula, and moved to headquarters site. Then, on the twelfth, we started operating a radar complex on the top of that hill we were going to occupy before we were sent out to Tori Shima. This large, semi-permanent structure had been constructed with a newer radar unit, more sophisticated than our small portable set. It didn't take long for us to catch on to the operation of it, though, as radar is radar. For this three-week assignment we were temporarily transferred to the 305 Fighter Control Squadron. Then it was back to Company 727 to wait again for our ship home.

Each day we lived for some word, any word that would hint of when we would leave Okinawa. One story was that a big shot from Washington had come over to speed up the transportation of army men. Since V-J Day, only Marines, Seabees, and other naval personnel had been leaving the island.

With word that the 727 was being de-activated, a final get-together party was planned. Gross and I got two guys from another company to shift scheduled time on the radar with us so we could attend. Instead of the six to midnight shift, we got midnight to six A.M. That being a much tougher shift, it wasn't difficult to get them to switch. The party was something of a dud for those of us who were not beer drinkers. There was plenty of beer, but not much else. We just stood around and talked with the same guys we talked with at camp and about the same subject—our transportation home. For the long ride back to camp after the party broke up, five of us piled into a jeep. Hartzeihm was at the wheel and having difficulty keeping to the road. He'd had his share of the free booze. We were in no hurry to get back to camp, so no one cared how long it took. All we cared about was the ship that would take us home, although Gross and I had to get up to the mountaintop before midnight.

Finally came the call, "All men with fifty-five points or more will proceed to the holding area at Machinato." Gross had fifty-one points, Hartzeihm fifty-three, Finnegan fifty-four, Dymond and Thomas fifty-five, and I had fifty-six. It was the first splitting of our group.

On December 18 in the morning, we got word that we would leave the next day. Then at noon on that same day, the word was, "We board the ship today!" We didn't need to pack since we had had our duffel bags ready for days. We were trucked down to the docks where we climbed aboard our ship, the *Marine Cardinal*. Two days later, at 7:00 A.M., the ship started. At 9:30, the ship stopped—a burned out bearing!

At midnight we started up again. We were finally on our way!

Chapter XVIII

The Golden Gate Bridge

We had crossed the finish line!

World War II had put our lives on hold. Passing under the Golden Gate Bridge into San Francisco Bay marked an end to a terrible existence that was at last over. The gate swung open, allowing us to leave one world and enter a new one.

Hostilities had ended August 15 with the peace treaty signing September 3, 1945. We knew then that, absolutely, no doubt about it, we would be home for Christmas. For so long we had believed that the war would not end until we had landed on the Japanese mainland and fought it out inch by inch, year after year, until every Jap had been killed or captured. It had been that way with so many previous battles, hopping from one island to the next. Suddenly, wonder of wonders, the war was over, we were going home, and surely it would be for Christmas.

With the agonizingly long wait, as one monotonous day followed another, we clung to every rumor while we scanned the waters, waiting for the ship that would take us home. With each step in the departure process we were moved from one holding area to another. Warnings not to leave the area were unnecessary since fear that we might miss a notice or a rumor of some movement kept us close. The long days passed so excruciatingly slowly that we wondered at times if life had not been easier when we were still in danger, completely devoid of hope, assuming that the unending war was our destiny. Playing pinochle, reading, and letter writing were only interrupted by meals. Censorship had ceased with the war's end so when writing home, we could say whatever we wanted. Before we had been so restricted as to what we could say. Telling exactly where we were and what we were doing and all that we had been through was so different that when writing it was difficult to believe we could say whatever we wanted.

As the days passed, "home for Christmas," turned from "absolutely," to "still possible," and finally to "not this year." When we finally boarded our homeward-bound ship, the *Marine Cardinal*, on December 18, we knew that we would be spending Christmas on the open ocean.

I wrote to my mother, "Don't take the tree down, I want it to still be there when I get home." It was a way, I think, for me to feel that Christmas would not be over until I got there.

As we left Okinawa, we were informed that our destination would be a return to Seattle, but once we were underway, it was changed to San Francisco. Posted on a wall on the ship was a big map of the Pacific Ocean and each day it was marked with our progress—miles traveled the previous day, miles from Okinawa, and miles to San Francisco. After two days at sea, with nothing in sight but water, the horizon in view all around, I looked at the map just after it had been marked for the previous night's travel. *Good grief*, I thought, *We've only gone a quarter of an inch and so much more water yet to go.* The statistics for December 22 read, "Miles traveled this day, 359; miles from Okinawa, 546; miles to San Francisco, 5,694; speed increased from 12.1 to 15.28 knots." Also, each day they told us that we lost one half-hour. As we traveled from west to east, the daily time changed. When we crossed the International Date Line on this return trip, we had two Fridays—two December 28, 1945.

C. S. Forester's character, Horatio Hornblower, helped to pass the time. The ship's library was well stocked with many of his books, and I could lose myself in the swashbuckling adventures on that other ship as it sailed through one novel after another.

At night the phosphorescence gleaming in the ship's wake had a mesmerizing, calming effect so needed to quiet our impatient anticipation. We were veterans in so many ways—secure, confident, so much older, so different from the young boys who had crossed this same ocean such a long time ago. I had long since conquered my seasickness by learning the techniques of movement on a ship at sea

The days passed one by one with just the blue sky with its small white puffy clouds and the even bluer ocean with its little crispy white chips, and nothing else in sight. Christmas was marked with an especially good meal of turkey and all the fixings. We wouldn't be home for Christmas, but we were on our way. It was also a sad, melancholy time talking with buddies we had lived with and shared so much. They were all family and yet, without acknowledging it, we knew, in spite of good intentions, we would never meet again. There was plenty of time, too, to get to know some of the sailors, young navy boys with less time on the water than what we had in the army. They were eager to learn what we could tell them of our war that had just ended.

Only once during our trip homeward did we run into some rough weather—December 26. Our ship rocked from side to side. As I sat at the table, having a cup of coffee, I reached for the sugar just at a time when the ship rolled and the sugar bowl flew from the table to smash against the wall. With nothing to do below deck, I decided to have a look at the angry ocean that was rocking our ship so violently. However as I stepped out onto the deck into the rain and wind, the ship's bow dipped and there in front of us was a gigantic wall of water that dwarfed our large troop transport, making it appear a small toy boat. I did a quick about-face and disappeared below just before that water came crashing down.

On January 3, we had a "rehearsal for debarkation." It was another one of those somewhat amusing army requirements—line up, take all your belongings, and walk down the gangway. It was nothing like the times with back packs, rifles, and gun belts, climbing down a rope netting strung over the side of the ship. For those times we did need practice. In addition to giving us a good laugh, it gave us that sense of being almost there.

Each day we watched that ocean map and absorbed all the statistics as that black line slowly moved across the great expanse of Pacific Ocean. Finally as the marker reached the other side of the map, on January 4, 1946, we got that long-awaited announcement: "Tomorrow in the early morning hours we will reach San Francisco." I woke that morning to a lot of excitement. My watch said it was 3:17 A.M., and when I looked about and realized that I was only one of a few still below deck, I dressed quickly and climbed the ladder topside. Just as I reached the top step and moved onto the deck, there right in front of me was the Golden Gate Bridge and we were just about to pass under it. Pandemonium erupted on the ship, with deafening screaming and yelling. I just stood there transfixed, watching until the ship passed under the bridge and all the noise subsided. Then my sore throat told me that I, too, had been yelling just as much as all the rest.

We had crossed the finish line. That life was over. Though the war had actually ended in August and I would not be discharged from the army until we reached Ft. Devens, the Golden Gate Bridge marked a passing from one world into another.

We sailed past Alcatraz and moved to a dock alongside many other ships where we waited. It was typical army life—waiting. We had assumed we would be disembarking shortly, but we got a cold, boxed lunch and then another at suppertime before we transferred to another ship to sail up a river to a place called Pittsburg. We hoisted our duffel bags, left the ship, and headed for the waiting trucks. It was getting dark and we were very tired after the long day. I noticed one guy on his knees kissing the ground. It must have been something he'd been planning for a long time.

We were US Army war veterans returning to the United States, but there were no trumpets, no drums, and no parade. But those thoughts never occurred to us at the time, so anxious were we that nothing delay our return home.

As I climbed up into the back of the truck with all the other guys, hoisting my duffel bag along, I caught just the tailend of one conversation. I heard the guy say, "from a town in the most southern part of Maine."

"Where?" I yelled. "What town?" I practically jumped at him.

"Eliot," he calmly said. It was obvious that I was interrupting his conversation.

"I'm from Kittery." It was the first time in the years during my army life that I didn't have to say "Maine" or go on to explain where Kittery, Maine is. I really was almost home.

The truck took us to Camp Stoneman, an army base, for more processing and to await our train-ride home.

A few days later our train arrived. Our accommodations were a converted boxcar with iron bunks. But for this last leg of our journey home, we would have been willing to walk. The rails were so crowded with trains coming and going that we were obliged to take a very circuitous route. From California, we went south into Texas, then north through Tennessee and Kentucky, and eventually up into Vermont before finally turning south to reach Ft. Devens. I got the feeling that they were deliberately delaying our return as long as possible.

Ft. Devens, Ayer, Massachusetts, was where I started my army life and where it would finally end.

Chapter XIX

Home

Once our train finally reached Ft. Devens, there was a mad scramble to get into one of the long lines at the telephone booths. Everyone wanted to make that all-important call, to let the family know, "I'm almost home." It would be a few days, they told us, to process all the paperwork with so many returning soldiers. We received our severance pay and were instructed to turn in any firearms we might still possess. The PX was crowded with many men buying small items they needed in order to spruce up their appearance for the family.

Each man was interviewed individually. One question, among the many questions that were posed to us was: Did we have any war-related physical problems that might qualify us for a disability pension? This question was followed with a cryptic annotation that it would require at least two more days before we could be examined. With this blatant threat, I doubt that very many chose to stay one minute longer than absolutely necessary.

My whole family—father; mother; sister, Virginia; brothers Bob and Mason; and Bob's fiancé, Fran—came down the next day and we visited for a while. They wanted me to call as soon as I was released so they could drive down again to get me. But that scenario would not concur with the way I had dreamed it would be. My fantasy had me walking up that street where we lived, seeing all the houses I knew so well, and then arriving at the door. Nothing was going to destroy that dream.

The next day I got my discharge certificate and a special lapel pin that said I was a veteran of World War II. The pin was actually an eagle, but someone called it a "ruptured duck" and that's how it became known.

I had sent my duffel bag home with the family so all I had with me when I climbed aboard the train was a small bag containing some toiletries and extra clothing.

To one so anxious, it seemed that the train stopped at every small town on its way to Portsmouth, New Hampshire. From the railroad station, I walked uptown to the USO building, which was situated close to the bridge that crosses from New Hampshire into Kittery, Maine. The club was crowded with servicemen involved in many different activities. These were men stationed in the area, mostly sailors from the shipyard along with some soldiers

91

from a nearby army base, fresh-faced youngsters who made me feel old. However, my only interest in the building was in the locker rooms downstairs. I changed into the clean uniform I'd carried in my bag, buffed my boots to a nice shine, and now I was ready.

Once out on the street, the first car that came along stopped. He seemed somewhat pleased to be giving a ride to a returning serviceman. When he learned where I had been and that this was the last leg of my trip home, he was so impressed that he was not just willing to go out of his way, but anxious to drive me right to the door. When we arrived at the end of my street, I asked him to let me off there. I made it clear that I preferred to walk that street. No further explanation was necessary, I think he understood.

There was a slight chill in the January air, but I felt warm as I walked up Woodlawn Avenue. It was suppertime, so no one was out as I passed each house. Everything was just as I remembered it. I wanted to run, but I also wanted to savor those last few steps, the culmination of a long-held dream.

There was the big white house. I was home.

Conclusion

While on Okinawa, my pay for the month was six hundred-six yen ($40.40)–that is, when the paymaster eventually got to our camp. I think the 600 was my regular pay and the added six was for hazardous duty. It must have been that way for life was very cheap. War tends to alter values out of all proportion to what life was like and, hopefully, would someday be again.

Until that day, the initial landings on Leyte in the Philippines, the day my war began, I had never seen a dead body. No one dear to me had ever died, except for grandparents when I was too young to know. I had never even attended a funeral. But on that day October 20, 1944, there were dead bodies everywhere. I had stood on the bow of our ship as it beached and watched Jap snipers picking off the bulldozer operators from their machines as they pushed sand up to the doors of the ship's bow. Their bodies lay there along with all the rest of the dead. In less than forty-eight hours we were witness to human bodies in all forms of decomposition. With some rigor mortis would have set in and the body would be in some contorted, unnatural position. One thing about war that cannot be conveyed with the written word is the overwhelming stench of death, an odor that seemed to permeate our very clothing. The flies all around the dead would literally cover the face while maggots began crawling before the burial detail could dispose of that human carnage. Many blue and bloated bodies would be straining at the ragged material still clinging to the corpse.

As the days passed, life and death grew closer. Not a day went by when there were not dead lying about. In one case, after months on the island of Leyte, we came across one overlooked human remains that was just a skeleton. The rags that still partly covered the bones were flapping in the breeze as if the body was struggling to return to the living.

The worst place of all was Ormoc. This site had been shelled and bombed so extensively that the area was strewn with human body parts. The only recourse the military had was to bulldoze all the remains into one of the big bomb craters.

Okinawa was not as bad for us. We had arrived while the conquest of the island was still being hotly contested but were not involved in the initial landings as we had been in the

Philippines. Yet it was not unusual to see a human body lying by the side of the road as it waited patiently, quiet and still, to be carried off for burial. Today, we would recoil at the sight of a dead dog or cat by the roadside, with more shock than we ever felt during the war at the sight of a dead human being. Life was different, and we were different because of that life we lived.

One bright sunny morning on Okinawa the body of an old man lay between the strands of barbed wire that encircled our camp. Somehow he had managed to creep through three circles of the wire enclosure before being shot by the guard. Within each circle of wire, the strands were very close together and had noisemakers attached. It was impossible for anything, anything at all, to get through that enclosure without being detected, yet there he was. He appeared very old. It seemed sad to see this still, rag-clothed body lying there just as the sun was rising—the beginning of another day.

In all that time during World War II it never occurred to me that I might not return. From the initial landing on A-day in the Philippines and through the battle of Okinawa, I felt that this was just an interlude, a time out. Some day I would be home to continue my interrupted life, although there were many times when we felt that the war was never going to end. Maybe a little of that confidence was faith, but mostly, I think it was that youthful assurance. But, I had more than just a little luck.

There were many incidents in those war years of my going beyond the limits of caution, not using good reasoning, and for that I was awarded with special recognition and chosen above others for difficult assignments because of what they termed "bravery." Actually, it was really foolhardiness, not courage. I was very lucky.

War is by nature a very dangerous existence. No one escapes unscathed. Yet few of the wounds actually come from bullets or other flying bits of metal. During those years, I had more than one case of dengue fever. I had yellow jaundice, ear fungus, athlete's foot, and many other irritations caused by the heat, the bugs, the humid climate, rain, and lack of food. So maybe I earned that extra six yen they gave me. Some of those ills are cured, but as it is with most anyone who has been there, no amount of pay will ever erase the haunting memories.

Yet even the most catastrophic event in life is not without some redeeming feature. Memories of war can never be erased and no one who has experienced it would ever wish to live that life again. Still, war with all its pain, suffering, death, destruction, and tears had some positives for me. I had a chance to be a part of history. I shared a life with others where dependence made differences non-existent. I saw and experienced things I would never otherwise have seen or even known about.

We think we know how we would react under certain conditions and yet not many ever get the opportunity to find out. Without being tested, we can never know for sure how we would fare. War was that ultimate test for me. I survived, I returned, and what the war gave to me was that chance—I got to know myself.

World War II

In the Pacific Theater

Never Alone—Until Admiral Halsey
Left...with Everyone Else

Personal Involvement—with Typhoons,
Filth, Cannibalism, and Body Parts in the

Biggest War of All Times

by

Harrison E. Lemont

Excerpts from the book:

From the first day that we had landed on the beaches of Leyte, we had seen so many dead. Dead in so many positions and so many states of decomposition, from dead that had just been shot to bones with only rag covering, the hot tropical sun causing the dead to turn blue and become bloated in only a few days. Flies in their eyes, their ears, filling the air, some bodies crawling with maggots before they could be buried. The stench was so terribly str and the bodies in such a state that one could not tell to whose army they belonged.

Jap landing barge at Ormoc

We stopped to pick up a group of Filipinos, just one of many who were operating in guerrilla bands, in the Philippines. The first words to me by one of the young guerillas, as he climbed up into the truck, had been "I ate a Jap liver."

As the days passed, life and death grew closer. Not a day went by when there were dead lying about. In one case, after months on the island of Leyte, we came across one o looked human remains that was just a skeleton. The rags that still partly covered the bo were flapping in the breeze as if the body was struggling to return to the living.

Concentration on major battles with numbers of dead, wounded, and missing-in-action, of downed planes and sunken ships, omits all the mundane happenings that comprise real Army life in war. Sleeping in a fox hole under a pup tent, with one Army blanket spread on the ground, brushing away the mosquitoes, the dirt at the head sifting down into your hair and the rain water creeping in at your feet, no water to wash your dirty, smelly clothes, athletes foot stinging and itching in crusty socks, slow healing sores from insect stings, straining to see throughout a dark night on guard duty, and days with nothing to eat; these are the true images of war. The physical exertions, the emotional stress and the mental strains, make up the day-to-day experiences of tension, fatigue, laughter, sorrow, and pain. These small happenings are clearly more real.

BRIEF SUMMARY of my movements during the war.

On October 20, 1944, A-Day, we landed on Leyte Island in the Philippines.

We quickly established our radar set on the beach just north of the landing site and began giving early warning of enemy activity.

The day before Christmas we moved over the mountains to Ormoc on the west coast, where we continued reporting on Jap aircraft activity.

When the island of Leyte was pronounced secure, we were flown to Okinawa, where we placed our radar set on the highest mountain on the island.

As more advanced warning was needed, we were isolated on Tori Shima, a coral rock 50 miles west of Okinawa.

At war's end, our platoon was the closest to Japan, still on that coral rock, still sending messages to headquarters.

Harrison E. Lemont

Natives helping us build a hut

Walter Lippman said, "War will never be abolished by people who are ignorant of war."

The memories of what we experienced even time cannot diminish. Some of those scattered pictures in the mind can never be erased. Unpleasant happenings we try to forget—it's proper to put them out of mind and move on. But what we forget, we are too often condemned to repeat. War even with all its horror and suffering, or more appropriately because of those horrors, must not be forgotten.

Our Radar Set

To acquire the book or for additional copies:

Call:
    207-439-6566
    435 U.S.Route One
    Kittery, ME 03904

or Write:

    Harrison E. Lemont
    P. O. Box 58
    Kittery, ME 03904

Cost of Book $17.00
If mailed, postage   1.42
                     18.42